Ade McCormack sounds a much-needed clarion call for IT to "grow up" and become a mature business function. And he provides a practical management framework and a rich set of case studies that will help companies achieve that difficult goal.
– **Nicholas Carr, author of *Does IT Matter?* and *The Big Switch*.**

"Ade McCormack hits at the key issues, the Business/IT relationship can no longer be one of master/slave, but must evolve into one of value based partnership for business advantage. An essential read for those organisations who believe there has to be a third way between traditional business and IT approaches."
"The IT Value Stack demonstrates that the management of data, information and knowledge is the competitive advantage battleground for 21st century organisations. Entwining business and IT across, Strategy, People, Process, Technology and Service will give you the tactics in this new battleground and move you onwards to delivering true business value."
Eddie Short, Vice President, Global Lead – Business Information Management, Capgemini, London.

The wit, imagination and insight that Ade brings to his regular Boardroom Debate column in the Financial Times Digital Business section shine through his new book. Ade looks at where the power, blame, influence and value in IT all sit as business technology matures and the game shifts towards maximising its value.
In IT Demystified, Ade explained how technology works; now he continues the deeper debate sparked off by Nicholas Carr – another FT Digital Business commentator – on the importance of IT to business. Ade has written a book ideal for those who like to take their IT with a smile and no mist.
Peter Whitehead, FT Digital Business editor

Practical, stimulating and challenging. Ade McCormack has produced a book that will enable business leaders to understand what IT can do for them and how they can build the organisational relationships and processes, which will lead to greater success. Alongside, his informal writing style and practical experience makes this book readily accessible and very enjoyable.
Richard Wyatt-Haines, author of Align IT: Business Impact through IT.

"I am passionate about raising the level of leadership in the corporate world and I draw heavily from my experience as a polar explorer. I have always sought to innovate and use research as a basis for action. A key message I take from Ade McCormack's book The IT Value Stack is that the skills needed for successful business leadership now embrace the strategic use of IT, in particular in the domains of innovation, risk management and monitoring the market pulse."
Alan Chambers MBE, leader of the first successful unassisted British expedition to the North Pole, co-author Keep Walking: Leadership Learning in Action.

The IT Value Stack

A boardroom guide to IT leadership

Ade McCormack

John Wiley & Sons, Ltd

Other Wiley Editorial Offices

John Wiley & Sons Inc., 111 River Street, Hoboken, NJ 07030, USA

Jossey-Bass, 989 Market Street, San Francisco, CA 94103-1741, USA

Wiley-VCH Verlag GmbH, Boschstr. 12, D-69469 Weinheim, Germany

John Wiley & Sons Australia Ltd, 42 McDougall Street, Milton, Queensland 4064, Australia

John Wiley & Sons (Asia) Pte Ltd, 2 Clementi Loop #02-01, Jin Xing Distripark, Singapore 129809

John Wiley & Sons Canada Ltd, 6045 Freemont Blvd, Mississauga, ONT, L5R 4J3

Wiley also publishes its books in a variety of electronic formats. Some content that appears in print may not be available in electronic books.

Anniversary Logo Design: Richard J. Pacifico

Library of Congress Cataloging-in-Publication Data

McCormack, Ade.
The IT Value Stack : A boardroom guide to IT leadership / Ade McCormack.
    p. cm.
  Includes bibliographical references and index.
  ISBN 978-0-470-01853-8 (cloth : alk. paper)
  1. Information technology–Management. I. Title.
  HD30.2.M394 2007
  658.4'038 – dc22
                                                        2007013731

A catalogue record for this book is available from the British Library

ISBN: 978-0-470-01853-8

Typeset in 10/16pt Kuenstler 480BT by SNP Best-set Typesetter Ltd., Hong Kong
Printed and bound in Great Britain by TJ International Ltd, Padstow, Cornwall

This book is printed on acid-free paper responsibly manufactured from sustainable forestry in which at least two trees are planted for each one used for paper production.

CONTENTS

Introduction: What's IT All About?

"Leadership has a harder job to do than just choose sides. It must bring sides together."

Jesse Jackson, US Civil Rights Leader

Introduction

Welcome to *The IT Value Stack – A Boardroom Guide to IT Leadership*. Before we get into the content proper I have provided some insights into why I have written this book. This opening chapter also details the book's structure.

I have my Reasons

Having worked in the IT sector for more than two decades, I have made a number of observations that are in many ways interrelated:

- The IT industry has a poor delivery record.
- Business people do not know what IT people are talking about.
  And this doesn't seem to bother IT people.
- Users are generally suspicious of IT people.
- Executives are frustrated that they cannot measure whether they are getting good value from their IT investment.
- There is a perception that all problems involving IT are *ipso facto* the fault of the IT department.
- The IT industry suffers from low self-esteem.
- Many businesses do not know what business they are in.

I will dwell on these in the next chapter.

Information Technology is not a Black Box

Whilst IT is an exciting (possibly too exciting) industry, it has a number of critical problems, which are both perceived and real. These problems may appear parochial to those dwelling beyond the IT department periphery. However, modern businesses are increasingly dependent on IT. As IT becomes part of the organisational DNA, these so-called IT problems will become everyone's problem. Thus, IT is too important to compartmentalise, and so does not fit neatly onto the organisational chart. Treating IT as a "black box" is not an option. Even aligning this black box with the business is not enough.

Information Technology has become Important

For many organisations IT was no more strategic than catering services. "Nobody died today, so why does the catering manager want to talk to me?" bellows the CEO. So it is with the CIO, "The email works so why does he want to talk to me?"

However, the world has changed. Users are in the driving seat. Regulatory compliance lingers like a dark cloud. The threats extend beyond the traditional boundaries. Global competition, cyber crime and terrorism require different rules of engagement. Tactics are the new strategy. We hear of on-demand, real-time, Darwinian, agile and other market-responsive terms to describe businesses. Information technology isn't an optional extra, it is a condition of entry to most markets. It is the enabler of business sustainability. The CEOs who don't get that are either in the wrong job or have done some calculations in respect of their retirement date and this reality dawning on the shareholders.

What Problem?

Business and the public sector/society are increasingly underpinned by IT. Unfortunately, many organisations are unaware of this. They can be identified by the lack of IT representation at board level. And those that do recognise the importance of IT to their survival are generally vexed by the poor delivery/value and the generally dysfunctional relationship between the users and the IT department.

A Deserved Reputation

Through my experiences working in the roles of technologist, management consultant, CIO coach, user and buyer of technology services, I believe I can see where the problems lie, and what needs to be done to resolve them. To that end I have developed a framework that encompasses what I believe to be good practice.

I feel strongly about this. I am not proud to be working for an industry that is held in such low esteem. Much of IT's reputation is sadly deserved. Reasons include:

- Socially inept technologists who seem incapable of communicating with the users.
- Unscrupulous sales people who, through a toxic combination of not quite knowing what they sell coupled with aggressive sales targets, will confidently tell users what is best for them.
- Technology providers that regard delivery as a by-product of their primary business, which appears to be sales.
- A mystifying deluge of user-unfriendly terminology.
- A lack of standardisation, both in respect of technology and terminology.

Every industry has elements of the above. If we look at it from a Bell curve distribution perspective, such occurrences are usually at the extreme. For IT, these reasons represent the norm, rather than the extremes. That has to change.

Grow Up

In defence of the IT industry, it is young and to some extent pubescent. So its behaviour can possibly be attributed to "hormonal effects" that are beyond its control. Well, it is time for the IT industry to grow up. Again IT is not a fashion accessory for twenty-first century organisations. The value they extract from IT will determine their success. Users expect IT to deliver, if IT fails to deliver then this will have profound consequences on the global economy.

The IT industry needs to get its act together. This is both a warning and an opportunity; particularly for CIOs who want to influence the business, and for technologists who recognise the link between user happiness and their career progression.

Snap

Without wanting to sound too visionary, I had a road to Damascus (actually to St Bart's hospital) experience circa 20 years ago, which involved a prolonged stay in hospital and four operations. Prior to this my IT experience involved some Fortran programming during my Astrophysics degree, and three years of real-time embedded software engineering at a large engineering company. This would understandably suggest I was a "hardcore techie". Anyway, my reason for hospitalisation was that I broke (snapped) my forearm cleanly during a judo demonstration (!). During my stay(s) in hospital I was struck by the skill, knowledge and caring manner of the medical staff. Nurses and doctors inspired confidence, managed expectations well and were consistently knowledgeable about their trade. It was at this point I decided that, despite the lack of professional standards in the IT industry (anybody can call themselves a programmer or a CIO), I would endeavour to be more professional. Specifically, in respect of my industry knowledge, which up to that point extended as far as my day job's minimum requirements. But I was also determined to improve my own professional bedside manner in terms of how I engaged with the users.

Over the years it became apparent that my initial observation, which was really me noting a need for personal improvement, was a problem endemic to the IT industry.

My Objective

Twenty years later my experiences of working with organisations at every level, across many industries, on both sides of the business–IT divide, have given me the evidence I needed to make what appear to be sweeping, and somewhat harsh, generalisations about the IT industry. But my objective in writing this book is to provide a positive way forward that will benefit IT-centric organisations, and make the IT industry one that people are proud to work in. An attractive industry will attract the best talent, and nothing less will be needed, given the importance that IT is increasingly playing in business and society.

But the IT industry doesn't exist to give IT people jobs. We are here to serve organisations and society. So ultimately those that extract value from their new technology investment will determine the industry's success.

Who is it for?

Well, I thought that if I really am going to make a change, I might as well start at the top. So this book is aimed at anyone who is in a position to make a difference. Specifically the book is for:

- Business leaders.
- Public sector leaders.
- CIOs.

What with governance being in vogue, those charged with driving good practice through the business and IT department will find this book useful. Technologists who want to entwine their activities with those of their customer will find this book helpful, as will users who need to lever IT to achieve their objectives. Technology vendors will find this book useful in respect of mapping their offerings to the needs of their customers.

Book Structure

The book is constructed around the framework I have developed to enable genuinely valuable IT delivery. The framework takes the form of a seven-layer stack, which I have named the **IT Value Stack**:

The book is divided into 10 chapters:

1 Do you have a problem?
2 Introducing the IT Value Stack
3 Strategy entwinement
4 Process entwinement
5 People entwinement
6 Technology management
7 Service management
8 Circulation management
9 Valuc management
10 IT value and you – the top 10

Chapter 1 sets the scene, and examines why the IT industry is underperforming. **Chapter 2** introduces the IT Value Stack model.

Chapters 3 to 9 expand on each layer of the IT Value Stack from the base upwards. Like all good stacks, the layers above are dependent on the layers below, so this ordering provides a logical progression. Chapters 3 to 9 each comprise four main sections, as follows:

1. Why we need to consider this layer of the IT Value Stack.
2. Why this layer remains problematic in most organisations.
3. What one can do to address this.
4. The perspectives of external influencers from both the IT and the business sides of the fence.

Chapter 10 draws some conclusions from the book, which time-starved executives may choose as their starting point. The book is as much a reference as an evolving story.

As mentioned, I have sought the views of respected IT industry stakeholders to validate the IT Value Stack. Details of the contributors can be found in

'About the Contributors' towards the end of the book. A Glossary is provided to explain the more esoteric terminology used in the book, which I have endeavoured to keep to a minimum.

Ultimately, this book exists to help business leaders become IT leaders. In an IT-centric world, IT leadership is a key element of business leadership.

Please Note

I have spent almost two decades identifying the problem, and have spent several years in developing the solution. Thus my opinions may come across as overly prescriptive or even didactic. The content of the book is well researched and validated through my own experiences through the input of industry and academic stakeholders. Unless you have not yet noticed, I will be taking an "emperor's new clothes" approach to conveying the message, as I think nothing less will stimulate action.

In this book:

- The term *user* applies to all users of IT, from shop floor to boardroom, unless otherwise stated.
- The term *business* equally refers to non-commercial organisations that are dependent on IT for achieving their objectives.
- The distinction between the IT department and the business is made to emphasise the cultural difference. In enlightened organisations the IT department is very much part of the business.
- Gender references are a sensitive issue in this day and age. I have tried to be almost random where sentence structure forces the gender issue. My use of gender should not be taken as a criticism/endorsement that one gender is more responsible for/suitable to the related context.

I hope you find this book both entertaining and valuable.

Do you have a Problem?

I made a number of observations in the introduction based on my experience in the IT industry. In this chapter we will explore these.

The IT Industry has a Poor Delivery Record

The IT industry has a poor delivery track record. Examples include:

- Ford's web-based supply chain management system. Abandoned – £200 m written off.
- McDonald's attempt to automate everything. Abandoned – $170 m written off.

Certainly, grand schemes do not appear to work. The much-heralded CRM (customer relationship management) systems, which promised to send sales skywards by consolidating the corporate view of the customer, are a notable failure. US analyst Gartner, at one point, suggested that over 50 % of CRM systems purchased were lying unused.

Recently, in *The Economist*, IBM's head of government services states that about 85 % of government IT projects are deemed to be failures. The problem of delivery is not confined to the dramatic. Mundane experiences such as lost data due to random word-processor crashes mid-document are common.

Why is it that we are so accepting of poorly performing IT systems, but are up in arms when a toaster behaves inconsistently? Is it that consumer rights do not exist in the world of IT, or is it that the IT user is not generally sophisticated enough to demand a better service?

Sadly, many individuals and organisations have become inured to the poor quality of the IT systems they pay for. Practically everyone has had a bad IT experience. I believe there are a number of reasons for this:

- The IT industry is young and is simply not mature enough yet to deliver technically sophisticated enterprise-wide systems.
- Information technology hardware is pretty reliable. That can be attributed to the mature engineering techniques used in design and manufacture. Sadly, engineering is a word that cannot be applied to software development. Unfortunately, it is the software that determines the value of the IT system to the user.
- Those tasked with delivering IT systems typically spend an adequate amount of time integrating these systems into the users' infrastructure, but spend little time considering how to integrate the system with the users and the business processes.
- Users are poor at articulating what they want, and IT people see this as an opportunity to increase the complexity of the solution. The user asks for a "mode of transportation". The IT department deliver a Ferrari – the user needs a bicycle.
- Information technology departments and the IT industry have little concept of public relations. They have allowed their reputation to become irrevocably and universally tarnished.

Information technology is too important to business and society to be in such bad shape. We need to get to a point where the term IT becomes associated more with innovation and value than risk and disappointment. Even professionalism would be a step in the right direction.

Users are Generally Suspicious of IT People

And the converse is generally true as well. Suspicion is underpinned by a lack of trust. I believe that as an industry we need to strive towards becoming trusted advisers, where our "customers" actually value our advice.

Very few technologists see their role in a service delivery context. The system administrator focuses on keeping the server running, the programmer is preoccupied with producing software in line with the constraints of the project plan. Whilst both of these objectives will no doubt be of benefit to the users, the emphasis on the technology suggests a "disconnect" between the technologists and the business imperatives. Thus the technologists are perceived as not interested in the business and thus not really part of "the team".

The concept of the IT department has done nothing to dispel this feeling. Occupying a different floor is bad enough, but being in a separate building or separate country is not the best way to forge deep and mutually beneficial relationships. The build up in enmity in the user community towards the IT department ultimately causes the technologists to reciprocate, which leads to a downward spiral in trust.

The emergence of roles such as systems analyst and business analyst is in many respects a "sticking plaster" solution to get around the low mutual trust levels between technologists and users. Their role involves traipsing the "demilitarised zone" between the users and the technologists.

The users do have more than a little justification for feeling this way. I have already mentioned the IT industry's generally poor record of delivery. But if we go back to the 1970s and 1980s, when mainframes ruled the Earth, printing a file was no trivial exercise. It involved submitting a "print job" to the IT department who would endeavour to give you the printout in 24 hours, but only if you spelt print correctly and used the correct form. The IT department was then in the "driving seat", and seemed to enjoy their position of power. The arrival of the PC was like a virus as far as the IT department was concerned, and this was a critical turning point in the business–IT department power axis.

Even if many businesses have forgotten about the IT 'service levels' during the mainframe era, they will remember with deep suspicion the Y2K problem, which proved the perfect excuse for the IT department to demand a bigger budget. Suggestions that the business would collapse without this spend, coupled with extensive media exposure, caused senior executives to play safe and not risk a catastrophe. Today, senior executives cannot be sure whether Y2K was a red herring or whether their spend actually averted disaster. This lingering concern still scars the users' perception of the IT department.

But perhaps worst of all was the dotcom frenzy. This is in part because the IT department was actually circumnavigated by the business. Something as funky as the web had to be owned by the marketing department, the head of which became the "new economy" head of IT. When the dotcom investment market ran out of "fools", the subsequent collapse burnt the fingers of many senior executives. Their self-loathing at being caught up in the hype was vented by effectively sending the IT department "to its bedroom" (aka severe budget cut) for several years. Clearly, IT was in the bad books. But whereas this was a justifiable view to have with the mainframe, and a questionable view in respect of Y2K, it was quite unfair to blame the IT department for the great "dotcon". Understandably, today the IT department carries resentment in respect of its unjustified and humiliating punishment

IT is Unmeasurable

Executives are frustrated that they cannot measure whether they are getting good value from their IT investment. They have generally steered away from becoming too involved in anything to do with IT, other than perhaps insisting that it costs too much, to give the impression that they are in control.

Sadly, most executives are not. Somewhat like advertising, they know they have to spend money on IT, but cannot pinpoint where the value comes from in their spend. However, they can sense value in that, where relevant, no advertising leads to plummeting in sales.

Eliminating IT spend would have serious implications. No email, for starters (though that might lead to productivity improvements as a result of people actually talking to each other). But many business processes would have to be undertaken manually or mechanically, which would invariably be more expensive. And forget about making critical business decisions based on the data you hold. You would be flying blind. So, it doesn't take much intuition to recognise that IT is critical to modern business.

But what frustrates many executives is that they cannot attribute a number to IT value. This can and does send CFOs into paroxysms of confusion, as they grapple to find a number, ideally financially denominated, to include in their spreadsheets. The problem is that measurement attempts tend to be cost-focused. For the CFO, cost is an easy measurement, and so is comparing costs with similar organisations. Hence, the emphasis in respect of IT measurement focuses on tangible cost rather than intangible value.

Any attempts by the CIO to defend the IT spend will be viewed with suspicion by senior number-crunchers. The IT department needs to help senior executives understand the value IT delivers, and do so in an executive-friendly manner. Much like in a sales negotiation, the buyer focuses on cost, and the seller rightly focuses on value. The CIO needs to move the argument axis away from cost. And to do so they need to have a mechanism for measuring value.

Perhaps most important of all, the CIO needs to educate the board in respect of who ultimately is responsible for extracting business value from the IT investment.

IT Problems are the Fault of the IT Department

Given that many users perceive IT as some form of mystical, if somewhat unreliable, phenomenon, it makes perfect sense to them to take the view that any system or business process that has an IT element to it is obviously cursed, and will at some point fail. In fact, this mindset can work well for the owners of these business processes. They can blame all process failures on the IT department.

Information technology is not always blameless in such situations. Misinterpreted specifications and over-ambitious technology architectures are just two of the causes of IT-driven business problems. However, many IT-related problems have their roots on the business side of the fence. For example:

- New CFOs who, needing to assert their authority over the CIO, insist that a given enterprise applications solution be used across the business. This is a mistake. The business should focus on "the what" (business problem) and leave "the how" (technical solution) to the IT department.
- The desperate sales director, who believes that buying a state-of-the-art CRM system will help reverse the fortunes of the sales force. A perfectly good technological solution is put in place by the IT department, but the sales force has no intention of institutionalising their knowledge by keeping the CRM system up-to-date. Can you blame the IT department for that, any more than you can blame the telecoms service provider for a poor telesales function?

Somebody has to take the blame when such situations arise. Again, the question boils down to who should be responsible. Business processes should have business owners. Therein lies the answer.

The IT Industry Suffers from Low Self-esteem

How many technologists do you see holding court at social gatherings, where the attendees represent a typical cross-section of society? How many of us board an intercontinental aircraft quietly hoping that we will be seated next to a technical architect?

The numbers would not compare well against a supermodel, a rock star or a sports hero. I am exaggerating of course, and there are no doubt very attractive and charismatic technical architects, but these are, it is fair to say, statistically insignificant. I hope that this situation changes. The more attractive IT people are, the more attractive the IT industry will be to the next generation of impressionable career-seekers.

More often than not technologists are not extrovert. Hence the IT industry appears somewhat introverted and uninterested in what lies beyond it. Not a good characteristic for an increasingly service-based industry. Introverts have their place, and in many respects are more grounded than their attention-seeking compatriots. That aside, in my experience many people in the IT industry suffer from low self-esteem. They have a sense that whatever they do it is likely to be disparaged by the users. Introduce yourself as an IT person at a party and you have instantly united everyone, in that they all have a story to tell about how IT has at one time or another let them down. Attempts to defend the IT industry by explaining that there are, for example, limitations to IP addressing, or that distributed databases lack mathematical rigour, seem to trigger laughter in those who bother to listen. The defeated technologist has just had his or her confidence ratcheted down a notch or two.

Such encounters create resentment, and drive many technologists deeper into their hardened emotional shell. The move to offshoring has reinforced the perception that technologists are a commodity. The value IT delivers would appear not to come from the people who build and support IT systems.

But what if tomorrow's technologists became the new rock stars, or at least the new business "Masters of the Universe"? A morphing of technologist to what might be called a hybrid-business technologist, with an impressive combination of technology skill and business savvy. Imagine an IT department made up of such people. Their ability to hone technology into business advantage would surely be more valuable than having an IT department that is more representative of a technology rest-home for the business-indifferent.

But look beyond that to a time when practically everyone at the party is such a person, it has become the standard across the business, and they are all laughing at the "old-school technophobic business guy". That day is coming.

However, the reality is that the nerds will **not** one day "inherit the Earth". Nerds, geeks, propeller heads, call them (us) what you will, are the result of a Darwinian split that came about with the birth of the first IT systems. These people were an "evolutionary" step from the mathematical sciences genus; mainly physicists and mathematicians who were attracted by the potential power of these "super-calculators" (aka mainframes).

The sophistication of the computers coupled with the unsophistication of the tools literally required rocket scientists to use them. Information technology has moved on. The tools today are much more sophisticated, and increasingly business-oriented. But Darwinism has yet to take effect on the people side. The future of IT, it would appear, rests in the hands of hiring managers and recruitment agencies. Choose these carefully and reward them well. They will determine your share price.

Many Businesses do not Know what Business they are in

This may seem like a harsh and inaccurate statement. And if you support Nick Carr's perspective that IT doesn't matter (*Harvard Business Review*, May 2002), then inaccurate would not even start to describe how off-the-pace I am. By the way, I happen to feel that Mr Carr's view captured the zeitgeist of the "technology nuclear winter" that followed the dotcom gold rush. Nonetheless, in my view it was an emotional rather than a thoughtful conclusion to draw.

My point therefore is that IT does matter, and it matters to the extent that IT is increasingly core to many businesses. What gives an airline its competitive advantage? It is not the type of planes they use or the service level of the baggage handlers, though they do have the potential to negatively impact value. I would contend that the airline company's competitive advantage comes from its knowledge of its customers and its ability to price in accordance with the market and still make a profit. This requires sophisticated use of IT. From this perspective, the airline business starts to look more and more like an information management business. Once that fact is recognised it makes perfect sense to:

- Insource all differentiating IT systems.
- Outsource all non-differentiating systems. For example, planes.

In such a business, there should be IT representation at board level. And the most successful organisations will be those that have a CEO who has come up through the IT department. This line of thinking is apocryphal to boardrooms of a certain age, but the iPod generation will find this much easier to come to terms with.

Another example is banking. There are many banks unaware that they are simply IT departments with a few retail outlets sprinkled around the planet. Those banks that are not big investors in IT may as well be in the property business. And those that are big IT investors, and thus have a greater chance of business sustainability, should outsource their real estate and concentrate on their core business, which will be to usher their customers online in order to continue making money despite declining margins.

When Bill Gates once pronounced that "banks are dead, but banking isn't", he wasn't referring to the death of the high street outlet, he was referring to the fact that if the banks were not careful their lunch would be eaten by more agile tech-centric banking intermediaries. Mr Gates' vision is unfurling. The major banks still exist, but they are increasingly being decoupled from the customer. Intermediaries such as payment service providers and account aggregators are pushing the banks into the shadows. Some banks may as well stop wasting money on their branding.

The smart banks are adjusting to the changing market. Those organisations that want to be the Pac-Man rather than the pellet recognise that they need to change their culture to be more IT-centric, so that the conditions are right to enable the innovative use of IT. For some organisations this is a thought too far.

Other Problems

Governance

Both private- and public-sector organisations are expected to practice good governance. In a perfect world every organisation would impose and adhere to its own high governance standards. Enron, Worldcom, Parmalat to name but a few have reminded us that it is not always the case. This has prompted external regulatory bodies to impose external standards in certain markets.

Sarbannes-Oxley is an example of compliance legislation, where the burden of adherence is significant, and the consequences of non-compliance are both deep and dire. Prison has become a hot topic amongst the boardrooms of many US quoted companies. Regardless of whether or not this legislation is an over-reaction to the fear that a lack of faith in US industry will lead to a collapse in the associated stockmarkets, it exists and it must be taken seriously. As organisations embark on the path to compliance they soon discover that the controls needed to demonstrate good governance are underpinned by IT. Thus the robustness of those controls is in direct proportion to the quality of the IT department.

Given that the IT department is generally treated as a "black box", then this moves IT from being an ancillary service of no great import to a major potential business risk. To establish the level of risk, the executive team has to open the lid of the box. And in many cases what they see will shock them. We all know the term engineering, and associate good engineering with reliable brands such as BMW and Bang & Olufson. In fact the IT industry contains many exemplars of good engineering practice, though the good practice is associated more with the world of hardware.

Software engineering is another story. Software, being more malleable, is generally subjected to less testing, with little to no design and scant analysis. In fact, software engineering has become a term associated with a narrow band of the software spectrum, namely real-time development, where the consequences of software failure are profound. Imagine a vendor having to recall half-a-million mobile phones because of a software glitch in the embedded call management software. Real-time developers practise engineering. The rest of the software market generally doesn't. In some cases vendors decide to let the customer/user inadvertently do the testing by releasing the software prematurely. This saves time and money, for the vendor at least.

Today, hardware is a commodity. The real value of the IT investment lies in the software. If that software has been thrown together rather than being engineered, then the quality of the governance controls is questionable. From my perspective, software engineering was abandoned in the 1990s. A more casual approach to software development followed. The IT industry will ultimately benefit from the increased focus on corporate governance, which has in turn spawned the concept of IT governance. In my view many IT departments will soon be trawling through their archived documentation looking for good practice manuals, which will in turn trigger a resurgence in "software engineering methodologies".

The IT investment needs to be managed with care. Reckless software development undermines that. Many IT departments have a lot of work to do to remove themselves from the executive risk register. My concern is that the opening of the black box, and the associated disillusionment with what is inside it, could trigger a new wave of negativity towards the IT industry which could trigger the next technology ice age.

Lack of boardroom voice

If the CIO was given a place at the top table then the problems above would have been less likely to fester. Most organisations have not grasped this and will continue to treat the CIO as a miscreant son, who from time to time is called into the library for a stern talking to. This has to change, though it is unattractive to many executives, given that the average CIO behaves more like a mature techie than a politically aware business-person. Such CIOs seem to talk in IT jargon, and talk in terms of IT projects rather than business objectives, profit and risk. Consequently, they are not welcome. This is a job for Human Resources (HR) – to groom the CIO to be equipped for the executive team. In fact, it would be good practice to avoid taking on a CIO unless they are in possession of executive DNA.

So these issues will continue to fester until the next-generation CIO becomes the norm rather than the exception. Smart CIOs have tried to catch the CEO's attention, as they recognise that IT has a role to play in creating competitive advantage. But trying to do that via the CFO, whose eye is on cost rather than innovation (which is defined as "a type of risk" in financial glossaries), is a real challenge. This arrangement must change.

Outsourcing

This lack of IT voice and a general disdain for IT has made it easier for organisations to entertain the idea of outsourcing. Globalisation has made offshoring a natural extension of this. But outsourcing the black box in its entirety may give the executive team a sense of relief, in that they have handed over their IT risk to an "expert". But as we have seen and will continue to see, this is not an intelligent move.

There are many reasons why this is not a good move. Not least when your core business is information management (see above), but also by outsourcing all your IT you have in effect put your corporate governance in the hands of a third-party outsourcer, as they now "own" your controls. Any CIO could have told you that, but not when they are several layers of management away. Over time, organisations will realise that only specific activities should be outsourced, and certainly not the business controls.

The mistakes of the board in respect of outsourcing will deepen the distrust they have in technology. Overzealous vendors are certainly a guilty party. The lack of strategic counsel in respect of IT is the real problem. The lack of trust between the CIO and the boardroom meant that any attempts by the former to flag this were misconstrued as an act borne out of self-interest. Such organisations typically receive their guidance from the outsourcing vendor.

Problems, problems

There is clearly no shortage of problems that reflect organisational mis-management of IT in respect of delivering business value. It would be too easy to blame the IT department, the boardroom, the users and/or the suppliers for this sad state of affairs. In defence of all stakeholders, the IT and business market have undergone seismic changes over the last 20 years. Remember that before 1993 there was no colourful World Wide Web and there was typically one PC per office as opposed to one per desk.

The IT industry has delivered the tools (weapons?) of the post-industrial era. We are in the midst of a revolution. Nobody is getting killed, but people are certainly getting fired, as globalisation, governance and the empowered customer demand that the bar be raised in respect of business performance.

Organisations are at varying stages of recognising the role IT has to play in remaining competitive in the Information Age. But even those that are evangelised in terms of the role IT has in their success, feel hamstrung by the lack of trust across the business–IT divide. It will take a lot more than a series of lunchtime reconciliation sessions to correct this situation. Organisations that fail to address this will find it difficult to remain viable as market pressures, coupled with their inefficient use of IT, take their toll. Countries/economic regions that fail to grasp this will become economic backwaters, though from a tourism perspective these locations will become areas of historical/archaeological interest.

So what hope is there?

I believe that there is a way forward, but it will require a substantial change in the way that IT and business interact. Previous attempts at this include:

- Bridging the business–IT divide.
  - Keep the two parties separate, even running on different clock speeds, but have intermediaries linking them together. This ultimately enabled the IT department to do its own thing, and from time to time help the business.
- Business–IT alignment.
  - Keep the two parties separate but endeavour to have them running at the same clock speed. This ultimately led to the IT department being told what to do without any say in the matter.

Neither has worked, for obvious reasons. I am promoting the concept of business–IT entwinement, where the IT department becomes a partner in the business and has a voice in the determination of business strategy.

Entwinement covers much more than simply promoting the CIO, though this would be a very positive start. As mentioned in the introduction, I have developed a seven-step process to maximising the business return on IT investment, which is underpinned by business–IT entwinement. There are no shortcuts, all seven steps must be taken. These steps are detailed in the next chapter.

INTRODUCING THE IT VALUE STACK

Overview

The IT Value Stack, see Figure 2.1, provides a framework for organisations to extract best value from their IT investment. It will help executives, technologists and users understand their roles in respect of IT value optimisation. IT service providers can use this model to align their offerings with the real needs of their clients.

In This Chapter:

- The rationale behind the model.
- An overview of the IT Value Stack.
- How the subsequent sections of the book are structured.

value management

circulation management

service management

technology management

people entwinement

process entwinement

strategy entwinement

Figure 2.1

Rationale

As mentioned in the introduction, the IT Value Stack has come about through my experiences of working with many organisations and individuals on both sides of the business–IT divide, in a variety of end-user and technology companies. My roots are in technology, and from an early stage in my career I could see that user–IT tensions were the norm rather than the exception. Working with business users and leaders reinforced my observations that there was indeed a problem. The tension was, and is, palpable at the boardroom and CIO level.

These experiences, coupled with my own frustration at the underperformance of my chosen industry, caused me to consider where the root of the problem lay and how this needed to be addressed. This led to my drafting the IT Value Stack, which again was based on my own portfolio of experiences. Whilst I have been fortunate to get a wide variety of experience, the model was still biased to my view of the world. So, for a period of two years I sought to verify the model through investigating best emerging and established practice and getting the feedback of power users, technologists, CIOs and business leaders. Through my own company, Auridian, I have also been able to hone the model.

To give the book more balance, I have included external perspectives on the subject of IT value maximisation. This might serve to strengthen the message.

IT Value Stack Overview

The IT Value Stack is so called because each of the areas that need to be addressed is distinct and thus they can be stacked rather than blended, so to speak. The stack model highlights the dependence of a given layer on the layers below it. Addressing a layer without having addressed the layers below will lead to sub-optimal value leverage. This is a key point, and a painful one. There are no two ways about it. If, for example, the Strategy layer is not addressed then one is building on sand.

By incorporating the word "value" in the title, I am focusing attention on value, both from a generation and a measurement perspective.

Like all good stacks, or at least all famous ones, it has seven layers. We take each layer from the bottom upwards.

Strategy Entwinement

To obtain real value from the IT investment, the IT strategy cannot simply be a response to the business strategy. The IT department needs to play a role in determining business strategy, and at times actually driving it.

Process Entwinement

The IT department needs to become business process consultants. This will increase the chances of systems being built that actually support the needs of the business users. It will also unleash value that no third-party supplier can match.

People Entwinement

Users and technologists need to be on the same wavelength. The generally accepted view is that technologists are at fault through speaking a foreign language that the users do not understand, which is largely true. However, the users have some responsibilities in this respect.

Technology Management

Much of the energy directed at getting better value from the IT investment focuses on technology management. My view is that it will come to naught if the underpinning layers are not firmly in place. However, technology management is where the "rubber hits the road". Without technology one can of course forget seeking value from IT. Given the inherent complexity of technology it can be considered an accident black spot, and if not managed carefully will lead to business failure.

Service Management

Many IT departments have put a service layer around the technology in order to protect the users from the associated complexity. The level of that service needs to be consistently high. Impressive technology with poor service ultimately results in a disappointing user experience. I advocate that the IT department should be run as a service business, and exist on an "eat what you kill" basis.

Circulation Management

The best IT systems in the world in respect of data processing will yield very little value if their outputs are not available to those that need them when and where they need them. Accessing organisational data, information, knowledge and even wisdom needs to be managed. The emergence of corporate governance requires that critical organisational information needs to be available to managers and leaders in a timely manner. I advocate a proactive circulation management programme, which embraces both structured data held in databases through to unstructured knowledge stored in unstructured documents and in the heads of subject-matter experts.

Value Management

Executives need to feel that they are receiving value from their IT investment. The CIO thus needs to be in a position to demonstrate this. There has been a number of attempts at value measurement, but there is a lingering sense that they are pseudo science, or at least inappropriate for IT value measurement. I believe that there are ways to meaningfully measure IT value, and they are simple enough to make value management possible. The role of the boardroom in this may make uncomfortable reading for some.

People Matter

Information technology value management is not a new topic, but today's market dynamics are exerting sufficient pressure on most organisations to force them to re-evaluate their use of IT and the associated value obtained. The thrust of my approach is that entwinement is needed before management can take place. And an underlying theme is that IT value management will be delivered by people as much as technology. Both are potential assets from a value perspective. However the people, in my opinion, are where the attention needs to lie. No increase in technology spend will yield IT value if the people are indifferent or even hostile to the notion.

Ultimately what is required is a culture change. For some organisations this will require extensive education, in terms of knowledge, skill and attitude. And for some organisations this may well involve a complete DNA purge if they are serious about being a long-term proposition. In these cases the old-school thinking may be so entrenched that extraction surgery is the only answer.

The world is changing for ever, and thus business leaders must bolster their leadership skills and knowledge to embrace IT.

Book Structure

It may seem odd to be detailing the book structure several chapters in. Whilst an overview was given in the introduction, I felt that it was more appropriate to lay out the structure of the core of the book once the scene had been set. Each of the next seven chapters focuses on a layer of the IT Value Stack model, starting from the bottom up. Within each chapter there are four main sections, discussing:

- Why the layer is needed.
  - The rationale for including the layer in the stack.
- Why good practice doesn't happen in practice.
  - What are the root causes.
- What can be done to address this.
  - The actions that are required to ensure that the layer in question provides a firm platform for the layers above, and thus creates the conditions needed to obtain real IT value.
- The perspectives of external stakeholders.
  - I have asked a number of influential people to share their views.

The structure is intended to enable the reader to use the book as a reference tool. To make the point yet again, focusing one's attention on a given layer will not yield full dividends unless the underpinning stack layers are under control. In this respect you are encouraged to read the book sequentially to understand the model in full before taking a scalpel to your organisation.

So, having set the scene, let us take a look at how to make good IT value management a reality. Let's start at the bottom of the stack.

STRATEGY ENTWINEMENT

> *"Strategy without tactics is the slowest route to victory. Tactics without strategy is the noise before defeat."*
>
> Sun Tzu, Author, The Art of War

In this chapter:

- The need for strategy entwinement.
- Strategy entwinement – why it doesn't happen.
- Towards strategy entwinement.
- Strategy entwinement – external perspectives.

value management
circulation management
service management
technology management
people entwinement
process entwinement
strategy entwinement

The Need for Strategy Entwinement

Organisations need to recognise the strategic importance of IT in achieving their objectives. A supportive IT department, which dutifully performs in line with strategic edicts, is not enough. The IT department needs to have a say in the formulation of strategy. In fact, as the world becomes more digitised, there will be times when the IT department actually drives the business strategy.

Strategic tablets

Good businesses set measurable objectives. These may relate to shareholder value, increased geographic footprint, creating new product/service, increasing market share, or any host of targets that are usually geared towards improving the condition of the investors. These objectives are given a deadline; they form the basis of the organisational strategy.

Traditionally, the business/organisational strategy drives everything. Approaches such as the balanced scorecard presume that the business strategy is cast in tablets of stone. The benefit of this is that everyone is mindful of what the business is trying to achieve. This approach also improves traceability in respect of who has to do what to achieve the strategic imperatives.

Similarly, IT strategy traditionally maps onto the business strategy "tablets". In fact, for a long time, the IT strategy focused more on the technologies that the IT department would adopt along with the systems that needed to be created/upgraded/integrated. All very important, but there was only the vague sensation that the IT strategy was actually supporting the business strategy. There was certainly no mapping of IT activities and business strategy objectives.

What's IT all about?

The notion of business–IT alignment has helped the issue of poor trace-ability between IT's day-to-day activities and the needs of the business. So today we have some correlation between business and IT activities.

Invariably, businesses have financial objectives, so it seems reasonable that the sales and marketing function, for example, structure and express their respective strategies accordingly. Similarly, building services will brace itself for the need to acquire further buildings or refurbish the staff canteen. Again this can be expressed financially. Building services and business development are mature functions. They have established how to define their metrics in a boardroom-friendly manner. So invariably the board is braced for the level of investment required.

Information technology, on the other hand, is not typically well understood by the board. So they have no real sense of what is an appropriate level of investment. Often the CFO will take a stab at the IT budget by trying to establish what peer companies are spending. Or will look at last year's spend and take the view that IT is getting cheaper and so simply strip a percent-age off last year's spend. These attitudes suggest that IT is a commodity and the focus should be on acquiring that commodity at the cheapest cost. But how is one to out-innovate a competitor using IT, if the IT investment is set to be identical to the competitor?

Officially, CIO stands for chief information officer. I would like it to stand for chief innovation officer. But as far as the CFO is concerned, it might as well stand for career is over. And unfortunately many CIOs feel that the latter acronym is actually not that distasteful and so are happy to accept their station in life. In any case, the CFO determines the IT budget and the CIO had better make do with it. This invariably leads to the CIO becoming a risk-averse, innovation-free cost-containment lackey. And so the organisation fails to reap the real benefits of IT. The CFO–CIO relationship is one of master and slave. And slaves are not employed on the basis of their advisory skills. Alignment is not enough, we need to move to entwinement.

An ideal scenario

Here is the ideal scenario in the business strategy planning process: The business decides that it will be the number two cheese-maker in the Netherlands. Instead of simply telling the IT department to create/extend the existing services to support that objective, it elicits feedback from the IT department in order to get buy-in from the CIO. The CIO requests that the IT requirements associated with the business strategy are defined in terms of IT deliverables. In that way, the IT department can use these requirements as business case justifications for the associated IT projects. Thus IT is better able to demonstrate that its activities are business-relevant, something that cannot be said for every IT project.

But instead of simply agreeing to deliver, the CIO studies these business-driven projects and establishes what the associated costs will be and what are the associated technology risks. The CIO then presents his findings regarding costs and risks. He may even present his concerns about the business benefits of any of the projects. Despite their clear traceability to the business strategy, he may, from his business-wide perspective, see flaws. The executive team then considers whether it has the stomach for this level of cost and risk. If not, it revisits the business strategy and concludes that it would be more appropriate to aim to become, say, the number four cheese-maker in the Netherlands. The IT requirements are de-scoped accordingly, and both IT and the business then proceed to execute the strategy with a good heart.

The business has now got genuine commitment from the IT department. The latter feels listened to. And as a consequence IT has little room for manoeuvre in terms of excuses for delivery failure. The executive team can now enjoy a degree of comfort, in that it is now genuinely managing its IT assets.

Competitive advantage

Let's start with automation. There are clear advantages to automating the business processes. Using commodity IT components to replace humans makes a lot of sense. Humans make mistakes, have aspirations and need attention. Whilst there is dignity in labour, it is ultimately more humane to liberate people from mind-numbingly repetitive tasks, so that they can pursue more "rewarding" goals. In a global market, businesses cannot afford to have flabby processes. So the choice is automate or die. Unfortunately, many executives see this as the primary reason for investing in IT.

Smart organisations recognise the benefits of investing in IT in order to make smarter business decisions. Market trends are documented in the databases sprinkled across the organisation. Evolved organisations have aggregated these databases together and have invested in tools to "mine" their "data warehouse" in search of market trends. If company A spots a trend before company B, then A can capture the market before B knows there is a market. Over time the companies that are most in tune with the market win. Terms such as on-demand, agile, Darwinian and real-time have emerged to describe organisations that can respond quickly to changes in the market.

Hardware is already a commodity, as are many desktop applications. But as the software used to automate business processes becomes commoditised, the competitive advantage gained from using IT will come from the sophistication of the decision-support tools, which are sometimes referred to as business intelligence (BI) tools. The market has a long way to go before business process automation is truly commoditised. The in-fighting between the enterprise application vendors will ensure that. And in any case, even if all competing organisations had, say, the same customer relationship management system, the one that had invested in integrating it with care into the business processes and had trained and motivated its users to use it would still elicit a competitive advantage from a commodity technology. Perhaps one day all businesses will have integrated their technology, people and processes with care. The degree of care will determine the extent to which competitive advantage can be eked out in a mature marketplace. Conversely, in a mature marketplace failure to address the above will surely put one at a competitive disadvantage.

So, how can an organisation gain competitive advantage using IT when the world matures to the point where everyone is using the same automation and decision support tools, and have all taken action to avoid the process and people integration issues? Up to this point in time, the focus was on how businesses can benefit from IT; a business-centric perspective on IT's role. I believe the next step needs to be an IT-centric perspective. Start with a technology and work out how it can benefit the business, which of course includes your customers.

This is not something that senior executives are accustomed to doing, with the exception of technology providers. At this level of spiritual enlightenment the CIO needs to be a partner to the executives, and to have played the role of digital coach to the board so that they have the knowledge to contribute to this IT-centric way of thinking.

CIO lacks influence

How influential were CIOs in getting the boardroom to see the business benefits of VoIP, a technology that significantly drives down the cost of corporate phone bills? Chances are that the CEO heard about it from his daughter, who was an early adopter of the services of one of the first-generation VoIP providers. This characterises the lack of influence the CIO has with most senior executives, and perhaps the misconception that corporate IT professionals, whilst okay at keeping the email working, are not in the innovation business.

Some of the big IT service providers have recognised the fragility of the executive team–CIO relationship and have side-stepped the CIO, who appears to have no influence in respect of the innovative use of IT. The board members are thus whisked away to attend lavish, all-expenses-paid offsite "disruptive technology" events.

This is a real headache for the CIO, who now has to contend or kowtow to the new IT directives brought about by a highly proprietary technology brainwashing weekend. The CIO–executive team bond needs to be of tungsten strength, if being exploited by unscrupulous but shrewd technology vendors is to be avoided.

The benefit to the business of hearing about the latest "killer-app" from the CIO is that he should be thinking in terms of what is best for the business as opposed to what is best for the vendor. Vendors are critical to the IT market, but their role needs to become less influential, and that necessitates the CIO becoming more influential.

So, if you accept that one day competitive advantage from IT will come from IT-centric thinking, then you must accept that the business strategy may not always be the starting point for determining the direction of the business. Should the CIO discover that advances in web–television convergence are just around the corner, the executive team structure should encourage this to be reported and the ramifications of this technological fact to be considered. Ultimately, the executive team may give it a "watching brief" status or redesign the business around web services that are sold and delivered to the customer via the television.

So, alignment is not enough. Business–IT strategy entwinement is the way to go. Remember, automation is for beginners and innovation is for winners. Actually, using IT to automate existing business processes is simply making the current business model more efficient whereas innovation through IT is reinventing your business in the light of what technology can do. Those that buy this idea accept that their business may look quite different this time next year. Generation iPod consumers will expect nothing less.

So what's your business?

One way of out-competing rivals that have access to similar BI tools is to have more data for those tools to mine through. The bigger the data warehouse the more likely it is to reflect the real world, and so business decisions based on the data are less likely to be flawed. On top of that, with more data there are likely to be more trends, and thus more opportunity.

Many of the New Age business books are talking about the death of the mega corporations and the emergence of the monofunctional niche players that interact with other niche players for as long as an opportunity or project exists. Certainly, the growth in small businesses supports that. But at the same time most industries are at varying stages of what appear to be parallel Pac-Man games. Globalisation equates to consolidation. Who are the Pac-Men and who are the pellets? Each acquired organisation adds to the acquirer's data warehouse and thus opens up more opportunities (i.e., synergies) as a better view of the world is created. Only organisations that have statistically insignificant data repositories stand a chance of being left alone in the race to own the global picture. Nonetheless small organisations should not take this fact as a source of comfort.

So, if the race is to have the best view of the world, then the primary business of the winners will be information management. This should give market leaders food for thought in respect of the importance of IT in their business. Over the next few years the organisations that have ambitions to play in the "end game" will reconsider what their core business is. At that point it may well make sense to sell the planes, retail outlets and factories, and lease them back from an organisation that enjoys baggage handling, property management or process control.

These are unsavoury thoughts for many executives today. But it won't be long before having the CIO on the executive team is a basic requirement of good governance. And having the CIO as CEO becomes an indicator of share price direction.

Rationale Summary

Business executives need to grasp the importance of IT if business sustainability is a strategic objective. In a fast-changing world, it is not enough to simply have an efficient and obedient IT department. The CIO has a role to play in driving business strategy. Business and IT must be strategically entwined. Innovation will come from IT-centric thinking. This will be a painful thought for many of today's business leaders.

Strategy Entwinement – Why it Doesn't Happen

As the world becomes more IT-centric it makes sense to increase the influence of the IT department over the business strategy. So why doesn't it happen? This section explores the obstacles blocking the path to business–IT strategy entwinement.

Techno-indifference

Many boardrooms have become indifferent to IT. For me this is more pernicious than technophobia. Like all phobics, once they are cured they often adopt a diametrically opposed mindset. Arachnophobes go on to become experts in spider behaviour. Haters of spreadsheets start to use them for shopping lists, measuring vital signals and Christmas card list management.

Techno-indifference has no pent up energy that, with a little neural reprogramming, can be channelled positively. Imagine you have taken up a new role abroad, where the working language is your own mother tongue. You start to socialise with your colleagues, but they prefer to use their mother tongue outside office hours. Initially they translate a joke for your benefit after everyone else has enjoyed it. This is socially awkward, and after a while your colleagues cannot be bothered to "socialise with subtitles", and they become indifferent to your presence socially. So it is with the CIO and the executive team.

It is likely that many senior executives are more technophobic, born out of the frustration of their own experiences with IT. But they have become so inured to this that the hatred has slipped into the subconscious, leading to long-term techno-indifference. The expectation management chasm that separates the CIO from the executive team is structurally prised apart by poor communications. Namely:

- The business jargon used by the executive team:
  - words such as profit, loss, governance and prison.
- The IT jargon used by the CIO:
  - for example, Gantt chart, TCP/IP, fault tolerance, web services, XSLT, Soap, Ajax.

Unlike the foreign colleagues mentioned above, the executives do not understand IT jargon, and are certainly not going to allow their discussions to be slowed up by some interloper speaking in a foreign tongue.

This indifference to IT has fuelled the view that IT is strategically uninteresting. Very few CIOs have convinced the executive team that they "speak business", and as a result there is generally very little genuine IT representation at board level.

The board cannot pretend that IT does not have an impact on their business. But much like they recognise the need for electricity, they would much rather let the supplier provide the service and not bore them with the physics. Some of the major outsourcers would have us believe that this day has come for IT. It hasn't. Unlike electricity, IT does offer the power to gain competitive advantage and unlike electricity, it is less reliable. So the benefits and the risks need to be actively managed.

The CIO as bottleneck

The CIO is traditionally regarded as the interface between the boardroom and the "IT spend". Usually the boardroom point of contact is the CFO. For reasons mentioned above, the CIO is left out of important discussions, often called into the boardroom when the subject of IT arises, as if IT was some operational detail that can be viewed in isolation. Thus many executives fail to understand that IT is the platform for the business and impacts every element of the business.

So why is this? Well, new technology is complex and managing technologists is like herding cats: CIOs who manage their IT departments well are exceptional managers. However, the demands of managing the IT department cause the CIO to be somewhat inward-looking. There is no time to think about competitive advantage when:

- A major software contract has deteriorated to the level that there are now more lawyers in the team than developers.

- Cyber terrorists are attempting to bring down the ecommerce-enabled website.
- The front office equity trading system lost the business $10 m today because untested code was accidentally released into the live environment.

In short, the CIO is under siege and his desk sits right on the frontline. Typically coming from a hands-on IT background, the CIO gets a little too involved in problem resolution. Human resources departments should be sensitive to this and equip the CIO with delegation skills.

For those CIOs that have got their delegation act together, when they attend board meetings they are often ill-equipped to cope with the encounter. Information technology is simple. Like binary: on/off, true/false, yes/no, friendly/unfriendly. But the executive team seem to operate differently. "They are friendly to my face but disparaging behind my back." "He said yes to my request, but has not delivered." More often than not CIOs are ill-equipped for the political playground that is the boardroom. After a while CIOs are happy to return to the "comfort" zone of the IT department, and draw the lid back over the "black box". The success of the business from this day forward will be determined by the influence, courage and political awareness of the CIO. For many CIOs this means an extensive training programme to fill in the softer skills that they lack. Some CIOs will simply not have the capacity to internalise these new skills. They must be replaced immediately.

A lack of trust

But influence cannot be purchased via a training company, though the tools to become influential can. It is no secret that the secret to being influential is to make people trust you. This is doubly challenging when the starting point is one of suspicion. In business, trust is established in a number of ways. Delivering on commitments is a good start.

Being empathic and stimulating empathy in others are key skills. The CIO needs to demonstrate genuine concern for the success of the business, and to talk in business semantics rather than technology syntax. Conversely, he must educate his colleagues on the challenges facing the IT department, so that they are more sensitive to the CIO's plight.

Improved expectation management will deepen the relationship – executives do not like surprises. Trust is a destination, the quicker it can be reached the better. With trust comes credibility, and with credibility comes influence. Once influence is achieved, the IT department will become a partner to the business, rather than a supplier. Such a move will provide a "barrier to entry" for hovering outsourcers.

Who's got the power?

Observers would be forgiven for thinking that the IT department is toothless against the might of the executive team, and as such should know its place. It does seem odd that prior to the arrival of the PC, the business tiptoed around the IT department for fear of incurring its wrath. I remember a time when one had to submit a request to the IT department to get a file printed. Woe betide those who misspelt the word "print" in the job request form. Admittedly this only applied to the few businesses that could afford mainframes, but it set the power pendulum swinging. On day one of IT, the IT department was in charge. But time has moved on and the pendulum still swings. Today, the business is in the driving seat.

But even today the IT department is not toothless. Though the CIO might appear to be politically naïve in respect of boardroom dynamics, some modern-day CIOs are very conscious of the power they wield. If this doesn't ring true, consider the following being brought to the attention of the governance committee:

- An audit trail of the CEO's romantic liaison with a member of staff.
- A list of the "extra curricular" websites visited by the CFO.

Vindictiveness aside, whilst it might not be apparent that IT is delivering business value, it certainly plays a controlling role in critical elements of the business infrastructure. In essence this conflict is bad for both parties. The current model of IT department and business as separate entities does not help entwinement. We hear slogans along the lines of "IT is the business", and so we should not be talking in terms of IT and business strategies as if they are in some way different. But the reality is that the power pendulum will continue to swing unless radical action is taken.

Outsourcing the IT function and so making the CIO redundant is one approach, but that flies in the face of acknowledging information management as core business. Entwining the IT department with the business so that the boundaries are blurred is another approach, which deserves consideration. This is easier said than done.

Costs and risks

Business leaders need to have a better understanding of IT. This is not to say that all senior executives need to have an intimate knowledge of middleware and machine code, but they do need to understand the process of building, commissioning and maintaining systems. This will enable senior executives to ask more challenging questions in respect of budget requests. Whilst the boardroom team is typically very conscious of cost, its understanding of IT costs is generally weak.

The same can be said for technology-related risk. Such risks include:

- Technology
  - For example, the risk of using new and potentially untested technologies.
- People
  - For example, our expertise resides solely in the heads of contract staff that all have notice periods of one month or less.
- Supplier
  - For example, a bigger player, who is more concerned with eliminating competition than evolving the acquired technology solutions, is stalking our supplier.

The IT market is volatile. An appreciation of the associated risks is critical to good leadership in respect of IT matters, which henceforth can be considered as IT leadership. Chief information officers have an important role to play in IT leadership, but most importantly so does the executive team. This is not happening.

Benefits

It is not surprising that most business people fail to understand the benefits associated with modern IT solutions. The suppliers and even the IT department tend to talk in terms of features. For example, the new solution will have a thin client front-end and will use 128-bit encryption. This means very little to senior executives. More appropriate characteristics might include "the solution will reduce the total cost of desktop ownership by X percent" and "the chances of the system being compromised by external parties are negligible". Many people who sell technology don't know enough about IT to get into benefits-based discussions. It is easier for them to read the features off the fact sheet (whilst avoiding eye contact with the potential buyer).

Benefits are of course easier to understand when the proposed IT solution maps directly onto the IT requirements, which in turn map directly onto the business strategy. Until the benefits of IT are fully understood by the business leaders, it will be difficult to measure business value. Today a CFO does not really know whether $1 of IT spend yields more or less than $1 of business value. At the very least this is frustrating, and increasingly it will become an indicator of poor corporate governance.

Sponsorship

IT people are generally well-meaning. Occasionally they will take the view that the business needs a new system, without consulting the business. There are many data warehouse systems in place that bear this out. For sure it is needed, but it should be the business that determines what data it will hold. What the IT department thinks is important to the business is not always shared by the business.

Traditional approaches to software development that discourage interaction with the users similarly lead to sub-optimal solutions. The system may well have a business sponsor, but they, or more importantly the users, were "under-consulted" throughout the development process. Again there needs to be crystal clear traceability between the business strategy and what the IT department does on a day-to-day basis. Technologists should have a clear understanding of how their role links to the business strategy. Plus, the system owner needs to be a business executive. The links between IT systems and business owners are often hazy, or even non-existent, in many organisations.

Problem Summary

As we can see, there are no shortage of obstacles to entwining the business and IT strategies. Many of these issues have had decades to ferment and crystallise. There will be no quick fix solutions. Geological/biblical scale upheaval is required.

It would be tempting to ignore this stark reality, that to obtain good business value from one's IT investment one needs to start with strategy. Most recommendations to achieving a better business return on the IT investment tend to ignore this. Such advisors peddle their bromides and rubrics to the technology managers. In this way one doesn't have to bother the business leaders.

Everyone, on both sides of the IT–business fence, has a role to play in overcoming the obstacles mentioned here. Getting everyone to understand that they are in the same team is a starting point, and that they would collectively and individually fare better hunting as a pack. Second-tier organisations should take note. The large corporations are conscious that they need to behave as one fierce competitor rather than a federation of in-fighting units. Once they have resolved this they will truly punch their weight and the Pac-Man game will move to the next level. Second-tier organisations, and "under the radar" boutiques, should not take the current market for granted. All parties need to get in the best possible shape for an IT-centric arms race. Nimble is good. Big and nimble is better.

Towards Strategy Entwinement

Having recognised that there is a compelling need to entwine IT and business strategically, and having explored the reasons why this is not happening in practice, we now take a look at what can be done to achieve strategic entwinement.

Flush the DNA

Staff will see no reason for embracing IT if the business leaders do not demonstrate this by their actions. Thus all attempts to migrate the business to a more IT-centric culture are destined to fail if entwinement is not woven into the strategic fabric. To address this layer of the IT Value Stack requires great courage on the part of the CIO and great faith on the part of the executive team. Change management teams are advised to plan for what needs to be a cultural overhaul.

A dog breeder's mindset is required in that it may take more than one generation of senior executives to purge the "genetic flaws" relating to techno-indifference, and to replace them with a positive – even hungry – attitude towards how smartly applied IT can generate real business value. Even if the new world order sits uneasily with today's board, your young thrusting managers must be encouraged to see technology as a key business tool. And to be conscious that a positive disposition towards IT is a boardroom entry requirement.

Similarly, tomorrow's CIO will have a more exotic career path than simply working their way through the IT department ranks, most latterly in project management. This is of course a good grounding for running an IT department, but it is not necessarily enough to become boardroom material. Forward-thinking aspirant CIOs will have steered their career path to maximise their exposure to other business units, in particular sales and finance. The top team needs multi-talented individuals in order to run every aspect of the business. The CEO, to be effective, needs to keep the top team compact, so polymath executives need only apply. CIOs that are business-aware and have skills beyond IT will be in demand.

Engineer the DNA

Let us look at what needs to happen to get the top team in shape for improved business–IT strategy entwinement. The needs of the CIO and the non-IT executives are different, so we will look at each in turn.

People development can generally be broken down into knowledge, attitude and skill development (see Figure 3.1).

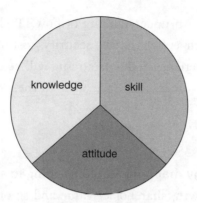

Figure 3.1 People development elements

Non-IT executives

Firstly, let us now look at the CIO's boardroom colleagues.

Knowledge

IT capability. Executives need to have a much better understanding of what IT can and cannot do. Specifically, this means keeping on top of the technology trends that may have strategic impact.

IT fundamentals. But to follow the market there needs to be a return to first principles. A basic understanding of the IT jargon, along with how systems are built, coupled with who does what in the IT department is required. This foundation knowledge will improve communications between the executives and the IT department. Also, where technology vendors break through the executive cordon, an understanding of the fundamentals, coupled with a sound knowledge of market trends, will make the targeted executive less likely to become a victim in the encounter.

IT value. Executives will also benefit from understanding how business value is derived from an investment in IT. Not just at the strategy level, but at every level in the IT Value Stack.

Business-driven IT. An understanding of how IT plays a part in critical boardroom issues such as governance, security, cost management, enhancing the customer experience and outsourcing will be critical to helping the executive see the day-to-day relevance of IT to their role.

Skill

Business–IT strategy mapping. It is one thing to set the business strategy in respect of growth, shareholder value and so on, but unless a direct link is made to the associated IT requirements it is likely that the IT department will become decoupled from the business. It is too risky to articulate the mission statement as a slogan, and hope that the IT department correctly guesses what is required in terms of IT support. Those tasked with formulating business strategy need to be skilled in presenting the objectives as a set of atomic testable requirements upon which the IT department can "hang" projects. The link between what the business needs and what the IT department should do then becomes transparent. Management of IT resources becomes easier with such traceability.

Business strategy tuning. In an entwined organisation the business strategy may change as a result of feedback from the IT department. Executives need to be able to balance the benefits, risks and costs associated with IT projects (which ultimately become services) to determine the extent to which the business strategy needs tuning in the light of IT department feedback.

IT department management. Good business–IT mapping as detailed above will make the management of IT much easier. It then becomes easier to identify and probe the CIO, when money is about to be poured into IT system development projects that have no traceable route to the business strategy. The exception to this probing includes hygiene activities such as network management, email, security and other infrastructure-related spend. IT spend is generally split between applications and infrastructure. The former (should) deliver business value, the latter should deliver the former. So traceability arguments cannot be applied to infrastructure. However, be aware that it is possible to overspend on infrastructure, so probing in respect of how the extra investment will improve the user condition will uncover misspending. Keep in mind that changes in business strategy will trigger new IT projects, which may require enhancements to existing systems or the creation of new systems.

But unless the intended business change is seismic, the bulk of IT spend will be in delivering the existing services, which requires investment in support. Thus executives need to be able to manage the IT department both in respect of development and support activities.

CIO development. Unless the CIO is treated as a peer, the impact of IT on business success will be muted. So, regardless of experiences to date with inviting CIOs into the boardroom, there needs to be a concerted effort to groom the CIO for executive-level success. Playing an active role in the career development plans of senior IT managers will be critical in providing the board with credible options for the role of CIO. But the journey only starts when the CIO sits down at the boardroom table for the first time. One of the more caring executives should be tasked with coaching the CIO to survive and eventually thrive in the boardroom arena.

CIO utilisation. Bringing the CIO on board is not a box-ticking exercise in levering maximum value from the IT investment, or to circumvent possible accusations of technology-ism (i.e., digital era political correctness). Executives need to have the skill to harness the CIO's knowledge for their own development. The CIO needs to become the boardroom "digital" coach. In the early days it will require skill on the part of the executives to extract what is really needed from the CIO in terms that make business sense.

Vendor management. Many IT vendors struggle to get past reception. Good IT vendors manage to catch the attention of the CIO. Impressive vendors get invited into the boardroom. By impressive, I am not making reference to their service, but to their skill in gaining airtime with the top team. These people are exceptionally persuasive, and have the tools to wow the most techno-indifferent executive. Ensuring your commercial body armour does not fall off is a key defensive skill. Being able to parry with the vendor is a critical offensive skill. The idea isn't to destroy all vendors that make it to the boardroom, but to ensure that those that do are credible and capable. Most importantly, the executive needs to ensure that the vendor offering meets the needs of the organisation as much as the needs of the sales person.

Core business. Executives need to constantly reassess the business they are in. Information technology in general, and the World Wide Web in particular, are changing everything. Technological advancements could soon consign your existing business model to the dustbin. Recognising this and acting early will be key to remaining in business. This requires more than an annual executive off-site to a well-appointed hotel. The market has to be treated like the weather. Every morning you look out of the window, and what you see determines what you wear. This analogy works well in the UK.

Attitude

Believe IT can make a difference. If lip service is paid to the importance of IT in respect of business success, then a poor return on the IT investment is guaranteed. Executives need to become evangelical about IT. This will have a cascading effect on the business and will accelerate the transition to becoming truly IT-centric.

Believe the CIO is a key member of the executive team. Experiences to date may make this a hard pill to swallow. But keep in mind you selected the incumbent, and it is your responsibility to make the CIO a key member. But first you have to believe this or the CIO will continue to sit in the dog basket waiting for the CFO to blow his whistle.

Believe that your business is under threat. "Only the paranoid survive" is not a bad maxim. "Pride comes before a fall" is also apposite. It is not enough to assume that you are doing well because the market is good, or similarly doing badly. The former may actually reflect underperformance in that with a smarter business model you would do even better. The latter may be a reflection that your model is flawed, and simply battening down the hatches until the next 'upturn' will lead to corporate asphyxiation.

Believe that you are an IT leader. Executives need to understand that the use of IT to achieve business results must come from the boardroom collective. Bringing the CIO on board is a step in the right direction, but every executive needs to become a business owner of some element of the IT investment and thus each executive has an IT leadership responsibility.

CIO

Let us now look at what the CIO has to do to be an effective member of the executive team.

Knowledge

Strategic awareness. Chief information officers need to understand the market forces that determine business strategy. This requires a new level of thinking beyond what is happening within the sandbags that surround the IT department.

Technology trends. As CIO, the executive team will expect you to be "on the money" in respect of the currents and eddies that contribute to the technology trends. The executive team will increasingly ask the question "are there any emerging technology waves that the business should be surfing?" Technology newspapers tend to be too low level. Analyst papers have a role to play, but an accurate vision will come from a variety of sources.

Functional expertise. It is unlikely that you will be invited to be a member of the executive team with a remit solely to manage the IT investment. Admittedly, more than knowledge is required to be truly effective as the head of – say – marketing, but being knowledgeable is a significant improvement over being clueless. The fact that you are in charge of IT means that your "client base" extends across all functions. Hence, knowledge of what goes on in the business is freely available if you simply engage with your customers beyond just order-taking.

Skill

Value assignment. The board wants value from the IT investment. Like a sage antiques dealer, you need to be able to assign business value to specific IT outputs. Chief financial officers in particular like value expressed in currency. Like all good antiques dealers you will be skilled at making the case for your valuation.

Influencing executives. Like the dawning of the Age of Aquarius, the business world is moving into the information era, which should be home turf for the CIO. Being sensitive to the preconceptions held by the executives and dismantling them through the creation of trust will be essential. Winning the board's attention is just the starting point. Helping fellow board members to see the wisdom in being IT-centric will make life easier for your CIO and his team.

Coaching executives. Ignorant customers are usually troublesome customers. Coaching the executives on IT matters will empower them to make smarter IT-related business decisions. Build a reputation as a digital coach.

IT department management. The headiness of working with the executive team may cause the CIO to forget that the IT department needs management. Good delegation and motivational skills are important. Knowing what to manage and how to measure it will ensure that the IT department focuses on what the business really needs.

Career assessment. Ambitious CIOs will invariably want to influence the business strategically, rather than simply take orders from the executive team. Such CIOs need to be able to assess the likelihood of achieving their career objectives with their current employer. The number of CIOs in board-level positions will increase over time, but for ambitious CIOs they may not want to wait around in the hope that their boardroom will undergo an attitude transplant in the foreseeable future. Ambitious CIOs will seek out organisations that recognise the value IT can bring to their business. Human resources departments, be warned.

Attitude

Believe you can make a genuine contribution. Having been treated with suspicion over the years, it is not surprising that many CIOs feel wary of joining the executive team. The boardroom is not concerned with charity (voluntary organisations excepted), and so will only have invited the CIO to join if they see the value in it (IT). Given that the world is becoming more IT-centric, the CIO's presence on the executive team will be crucial to the success of the business. But you need to believe it.

Be an evangelist. Embrace sales. The CIO needs to sell IT and what it can do for the organisation, at every level. This does not mean becoming a "larger than life" celebrity techie. It does mean taking every opportunity to inform the business of the role the IT department can play in business success, and tuning that message to the needs of the listener, whether they be executives, managers or operatives.

Be a business leader. Chief information officers need to break the shackled thinking of being just IT department managers. A business leader mindset is an entry condition to the boardroom, it will also make the transition to CEO easier when the time comes.

Be generous. This may sound a little like New Age thinking. But remember that the CIO, in being offered a boardroom position, has been invited to someone else's party. And the duration of the stay will be determined by what the CIO brings along. So look out for opportunities to help other executives. Nothing altruistic here, opportunities to support colleagues in respect of their departmental responsibilities will provide the CIO with an accelerated primer on who really runs each part of the business. By giving in this manner the CIO is acquiring the experiences that are needed to be a key member of a small multi-talented team. Thinking the unthinkable coupled with plugging into the "influence network" across the business will make the transition to CEO less of a corporate shock.

Action Summary

Business–IT strategy entwinement is the foundation of successful IT value management. However, it requires a disruptive amount of change at the boardroom level. Knowledge, skill and attitude changes are required across all senior executives on either side of the business–IT chasm. Some organisations will not be ready for it. Those that are have taken a peek into the future and are preparing themselves accordingly.

Those that intend to extract more value from their IT investment need to make strategy entwinement job number one.

Strategy Entwinement – External Perspectives

This section provides an alternative view to my own in respect of strategy entwinement. The contributors were asked to answer one or more of the following questions:

- Why is strategy entwinement important?
- Why is this not generally being addressed?
- What are the underlying problems?
- What are the consequences of failing to address this issue?
- What advice would you give in respect of strategy entwinement?

Why is strategy entwinement important?

When devising a plan to gain a competitive edge and succeed in business, technology needs to be part of the strategy blueprint – not an afterthought. Boards need to host collaborative business environments where strategy, finance and technology experts harmoniously co-exist. Joining diverse expertise and experience can yield optimal solutions that bring new products and services to market, grow business to new levels and deliver higher shareholder returns.

Heidi Sinclair, CEO Europe, Burson-Marsteller

IT is the same as any other function in the business. If it is not utilised correctly it is undervalued. Like all other functions there is a varying degree of commitment and interest in IT depending on the company and industry culture. For example, a small successful building business may not wish to spend millions on IT. If it did it probably would no longer be successful, and therefore has a conservative budget. Whereas the London Stock Exchange sees and treats IT in a completely different light. Like everything in life it's a question of balance and understanding.

Vivian Ash, Group Information Manager, BASF

The prevailing view from the New Economy was that strategy was dead. Organisations were no longer expected to set out their medium to long-term strategic objectives and follow them. Instead it was fashionable to provide direction on the fly without any consideration of its effects on the organisation's stability or profitability. Such an attitude to strategy led many organisations to rush headlong into investing heavily in technology, be it e-commerce or mobile telephony. Although some have been successful, the majority have not and vast sums of money have been wasted in the process. It is premature to write off strategy as it remains an essential part of any organisational planning process. Without it, it is impossible to make decisions that make sense in the medium-term or to test out investment decisions. Furthermore, without it, it becomes impossible to understand where best to invest in IT. The fact that organisations are now dependent on IT should come as no surprise to anyone. What should come as a surprise is that relatively few organisations manage their IT as a strategic resource and even fewer actively set IT strategies.

Andrew Holmes, Director, PWC

Strategy entwinement between IT and the business is important because IT is the guardian of substantial corporate assets in the infrastructure and systems it maintains. This asset base typically requires that a long-term (i.e., 3–5 years minimum) view needs to be taken and these timescales are often longer than the organisation's business horizon. Getting the IT investment decision wrong means that the business, at best, wastes money and, at worst, becomes constrained by its IT and misses important opportunities or is hampered in their exploitation.

Richard Boreham, IT Strategy, Governance and Performance Practice Leader, KPMG

Most business improvement (change) requires technology to lead or assist the change. Where technology is not considered as part of the change process there is a danger the technology benefits will not be maximised or worse the change will fail.

Nick Leake, Director of Operations and Infrastructure, ITV

No car production company would launch a new model without understanding how it will build the thing. Yet many business development areas will spend months locked away coming up with new ideas, which simply take too long to get to the market. Rather than admitting that they did not involve the right people, it can be simpler to say that IT could not deliver on time.

Conversely IT professionals need to learn to roll with the rough and tumble of finding solutions to business problems.

In summary, to not entwine business and IT strategy is to under exploit the opportunities to gain a sustainable competitive advantage.

Philip Wright, Corporate Services Director,
Standard Life Healthcare

The IT industry in broad terms is now "business led" rather than "technology led". Clients and business users want IT to underpin a business solution that delivers a return on investment for the business. The CIO should have a key influential role at the top of any company that wants to maximise its competitiveness and efficiency as a business.

Steve Tyler, UK Programmes Director, LogicaCMG

Why is this not generally being addressed?

First it is essential to recognise that IT is strategic and not something that can be ignored. And it certainly can't be pushed to the periphery of the organisation. Although it has long been accepted that IT should be fully integrated with the business, organisations continue to struggle with how to achieve this. They also struggle with how to manage their IT resource, assuming that they can leave it in the hands of the technologists and act as an innocent bystander as it disrupts the status quo. Successful organisations are those that allow the business to control IT, not the other way around.

The strategy for Information Technology and Information Systems fits within the wider context of:

- Business strategy.
- The execution of change within organisations.
- The way in which its application meets the demands of its customers and suppliers through its frontline operational staff.

However, many organisations fail to set strategy, instead aiming to motivate their employees through an inspiring vision. Unfortunately this creates what I term a leap of faith. This leap of faith has major implications for technology management and ensuring that the business is able to use its technology both effectively and efficiently. Such problems include:

- The inability to direct IT investments where they are needed most.
- No way of understanding how IT is adding value to the business either from an operational or strategic sense.
- Inability to control the costs associated with IT, as investments become a free for all.
- Visibility and importance of the IT infrastructure is lost and may be underdeveloped, thereby impacting the organisation's ability to meet its internal and external demands.

Andrew Holmes, Director, PWC

Assuming that the IT organization understands that the IT strategy should be aligned with business goals and that the goals are sufficiently stated, the next major challenge is understanding the diverse and varied *business* ways that goals can be achieved. For example, does IT understand cost drivers and ways to reduce them? In addition, does IT understand the following:

- How to create competitive differentiation;
- Revenue growth strategies;
- Sources of competitive advantage;
- Achieving product superiority;
- Leveraging intellectual capital;
- Growing the capabilities of the firm?

Without knowledge of how the business achieves its goals, how can the IT department possibly figure out the value-added role that IT can play?

Pete DeLisi, Founder and President, Organizational Synergies

A significant factor here is the different planning attitudes that exist in many businesses. Few businesses (other than perhaps heavy engineering and petrochemical) have multi-year planning horizons. Most are far more opportunistic following a general direction (e.g., brand exploitation or product innovation) and then evolving the specific business activities over a short period. Typical here are the financial and service industries (including public services). Contrast this with the typical wish of IT management, who want or need to know what infrastructure and systems to invest in and develop over a longer period, because of inherent lead times.

An example of the above is the frustration expressed by IT executives who complain that the business "does not have a strategy". Generally this means the business does not have a detailed plan that they can either influence proactively or develop firm plans against in a reactive sense. In reality, when business executives are approached, it becomes clear that both they and the organisation do have a strategy – but it is expressed in terms of broad themes, with detailed plans being restricted to the annual budget cycle. Unless IT can recognise and adapt to this, there is little hope for "entwinement". The business will only adapt to IT horizons where it has no choice and this is inevitably then a business constraint.

Richard Boreham, IT Strategy,
Governance and Performance Practice Leader, KPMG

Both sides are scared of looking ignorant and it is too much like hard work for both!

Philip Wright, Corporate Services Director,
Standard Life Healthcare

Technology is thought to be simple.

Nick Leake, Director of Operations and Infrastructure, ITV

What are the underlying problems?

Which should come first – business strategy or IT strategy? In the past, strategy was a relatively straightforward question to answer, but the impact of globalisation, technological change and e-commerce has served to cloud the issue. In many respects this is a chicken-and-egg situation because in some cases the business cannot define one without simultaneously defining the other. Normally business strategy comes before IT strategy, as the IT strategy should be linked to the overall strategy of the organisation; after all, IT should be aligned to the business. Even when organisations have cracked this conundrum, they often fail to keep their strategies up to date, which defeats the purpose of having a strategy in the first place.

I believe that business and IT strategies should be developed in conjunction with each other. In this way both can inform the other. Therefore, the best way to develop strategy is iteratively using the business strategy to inform the IT strategy and the IT strategy to inform the business strategy. And, because strategy cannot be developed in a vacuum, it is essential that the operational and technical infrastructures are taken into consideration. Failing to consider the operating environment, which includes the current IT systems and infrastructure, leads to problems down stream with such things as incompatible software systems, bottlenecks and network failures and incorrectly specified hardware requirements.

Andrew Holmes, Director, PWC

Technology is actually complex.

Nick Leake, Director of Operations and Infrastructure, ITV

Finding a common language.

Philip Wright, Corporate Services Director,
Standard Life Healthcare

Information technology departments are often staffed by highly capable but strongly technical staff who are happiest becoming experts on the software of a particular business application, or its underlying hardware and network infrastructure, rather than developing the strong personal communication skills to deal with business users or clients in terms they will understand. This just reinforces that IT is often seem as subservient to business strategy rather than being an integral part of the strategy at the point the strategy is formulated. It is important that the business sees the CIO as an equal and that that appointment reflects a mature combination of business skills as well as IT awareness.

The IT department needs:

- A mix of general management skills.
- Financial planning and management skills.
- Project and programme management skills.
- Business analysis IT skills.
- Good software and IT engineering skills.

Steve Tyler, UK Programmes Director, LogicaCMG

What are the consequences of failing to address this issue?

From my experience, there are a number of indicators that suggest that an organisation is flying blind with respect to IT. These are:

- Financial surprises on the IT side.
  - Investment, cost and budget overruns.
- No adequate support of the business and poor IT performance.
- Inadequate or late information on general business and operational performance issues.
- Standard processes, which take an abnormal amount of time.
  - For example, best in class in financial consolidation is 24–48 hours after month-end, quarter or even year-end closing. Some companies take weeks or months over this process, which normally alludes to IT problems either within local ledger systems or the consolidation system itself.
- Poor IT project delivery due to:
  - lack of business understanding;
  - lack of skills;
  - poor project management training and so on.
- Cry for outsourcing. Outsourcing decisions are often made without taking due consideration of IT's importance to the business and of its current health. It is often seen as an easy answer to the problems of poor performance.
- Shortage or short retention of IT staff and/or a relatively high number of external staff/contractors. This is especially critical when commodity type work such as computer operations is run with a high number of external staff.

- Tool or technical driven solutions from the IT side, which is often the result of silver bullet thinking; assuming that a single system will resolve the business's problems.

The root of these problems is a lack of strategic fit between business and IT, or a lack of integration between business and IT strategy.

Andrew Holmes, Director, PWC

IT alignment will not improve until IT executives start to understand strategy as well as, or better than, the business executives with whom they deal. Years of software package development in the marketplace has given them the false confidence that all they need do is propose one of the many packages that are available. Instead, they need to demonstrate an in-depth understanding of the various high-level ways that a business goes about achieving its business goals. Then, and only then, can IT proactively suggest ways that the IT resource can play a pivotal role in helping the organization achieve these goals. If they are able to do this, IT executives will be able to earn a seat at the executive table, and hopefully, we can at long last see IT alignment drop off the list of top IT concerns.

Pete DeLisi, Founder and President, Organizational Synergies

Failure or sub-optimal benefits.

Nick Leake, Director of Operations and Infrastructure, ITV

IT is today at the heart of nearly all businesses, just like electricity and plumbing is at the heart of all households. If you don't plan from the outset how the services are going to be arranged when you build a house then the house is likely to be functionally sub-optimal. If you don't embrace IT in formulating business strategy then the business will not deliver to its full potential.

Steve Tyler, UK Programmes Director, LogicaCMG

What advice would you give in respect of strategy entwinement?

The Head of IT/CIO needs to be a businessman first and foremost. He also needs skills that allow him to build relationships, lead highly successful change programmes and think strategically about what will deliver competitive advantage. Too often CIOs are technical based managers, their affinity with solutions loses them credibility with business peers and they are thus excluded from strategy design forums.

IT is no longer about technical solutions, launching technical platforms, etc. – it is more about enabling business change – changing the way we deliver in order to be faster, cheaper or better than our competitors.

Karen Mellor, IT Capability Associate Director, Astra Zeneca

A good IT steering group – proactive, knowledgeable and creative. The team being made of equal numbers from both business and IT.

Vivian Ash, Group Information Manager, BASF

IT is viewed as an investment at Alliance Boots. As such IT needs to make a direct contribution to shareholder value, whether that be in improved efficiency or uncovering new sources of growth. In a mature industry such as retail, there is a temptation to take the view that the business is "ex-growth" and so manage it accordingly. Our executive team has chosen not to become locked into this thinking. We are aggressively focusing on improving the customer proposition through a number of initiatives including what might be termed a "heavy investment in pricing". The strategic imperative of improved service at lower cost can only be achieved through the intelligent application of IT. I would thus advise organisations to ensure that there is a clear link between the business strategy and that of the IT department. When IT is so strategically entwined in the fortunes of the business, it is critical that the trust levels are high between the CIO and the other members of the executive team.

Rob Fraser, IT Director, Alliance Boots

An IT strategy can be considered to be an amalgam of a number of substrategies, which, when brought together, define how the organisation is going to respond to the business challenges it faces. It should address the following:

- The external business environment and how the business has decided to respond. This will be influenced by the core discipline of the business. So if it is customer intimate, the core information requirement will be around customers. If it is product leading, it will be around the product development processes and how well its products are performing in the market place. The information strategy must come before the information systems strategy, as this will define what types of information system are required by the business.

- The information systems strategy, which sets out the key applications that are required by the business to deliver the business strategy. This is typically written in high level terms and will outline those systems that are currently in place, those that require updating and those that have yet to be developed.

- The technology strategy, which covers the detailed aspects of the organisation's technology. As expected this will go to a much greater level of detail than the information systems strategy and cover the changes that will be made to the infrastructure, such as the communications network, what platforms the organisation is intending to standardise on, what office automation and email packages it intends to use and so on. This needs to take into account the current IT environment.

- The standards and protocols, which will be applied in the governance of IT. This covers such things as how new investments will be appraised, what quality standards apply to software development, what securities and controls are required and how they will be reviewed.

- The portfolio of projects and programmes that will implement the strategy. This will typically identify the relative timing of the initiatives, the dependencies between them, the broad costs associated with their implementation and the expected benefits they will provide to the business.

Andrew Holmes, Director, PWC

The executive committee and boards of companies should include a CIO role, where the CIO has rounded business and business management skills as well as professional IT management skills.

Steve Tyler, UK Programmes Director, LogicaCMG

How does the IT organization achieve this IT alignment? My experience suggests that the CIO needs to initiate a process in which he comes together with the entire senior executive staff in a setting that creatively couples the IT strategy with the strategy of the enterprise.

Pete DeLisi, Founder and President, Organizational Synergies

"Agility" and "flexibility" are used frequently within IT departments in terms of creating an IT environment that can meet business demands (at an affordable cost). However the IT department often forgets that flexibility and agility within IT are needed to support flexible and agile businesses. For IT the agility needs to be not just in the technology layer but also in:

- Management attitude.
- Creation of services.

- Structuring of the IT supply chain (internal and outsourced elements).
- The engagement processes (IT governance) between IT and its business customers.

Richard Boreham, IT Strategy, Governance and Performance
Practice Leader, KPMG

Encourage both sides to learn something of the other's discipline and challenges. Executives usually invest in finance courses, strategy courses, marketing courses and such like. How many attend IT courses?

Philip Wright, Corporate Services Director,
Standard Life Healthcare

Think about the technology elements upfront with the technologists.

Nick Leake, Director of Operations and Infrastructure, ITV

What other related points would you like to add?

Ultimately, the profile of the CIO depends on the strategic role of IT. However as IT takes on a more important role within the business, the need to have someone looking strategically at IT is essential. However times are changing. CIOs have to widen their capabilities to focus much more on the strategic management of IT rather than the narrowly defined operational role they have taken to date. To that end an increasing number of organisations are recognising that the task of the CIO cannot be fulfilled within a single person and are introducing another role; the chief technology officer (CTO). The CTO's responsibilities lie in the operational domain, freeing up the CIO to take on the strategically important role at board level. A more comfortable arrangement with the CEO and CIO looking externally and to the future and the CTO and chief operating officer (COO) looking internally and ensuring the business is operationally both effective and efficient.

Andrew Holmes, Director, PWC

Most major change programmes require multiple disciplines to work together. Typically Finance, HR, Marketing and Technology. Make sure they are all included and managed appropriately.

Nick Leake, Director of Operations and Infrastructure, ITV

PROCESS ENTWINEMENT

> "*Good people do not need laws to tell them to act responsibly, while bad people will find a way around the laws.*"
>
> Plato, Philosopher

In this chapter:

- The need for process entwinement.
- Process entwinement – why it doesn't happen.
- Towards process entwinement.
- Process entwinement – external perspectives.

value management

circulation management

service management

technology management

people entwinement

process entwinement

strategy entwinement

The Need for Process Entwinement

Organisational efficiency and effectiveness are largely proportional to the quality of the business processes. The automation of these processes using IT is commonplace. However, many organisations are failing to lever the full power of IT in process automation and as a result are not getting best value from their IT investment. This section explores the importance of process–IT entwinement.

People–process–technology

This trinity (see Figure 4.1) is the staple starting point for many management–consulting engagements. It is indeed sensible to consider the interactions of these three critical elements. Here we will deal with the process–technology interaction.

In keeping with my theme expressed in earlier chapters, aligning business processes and IT is not enough. Usually, alignment means that the technology needs to support the business processes, with no consideration of how IT might determine the business processes. The IT department is thus forced to take the view that the customer is always right, even when they

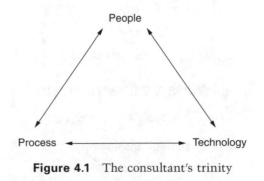

Figure 4.1 The consultant's trinity

are clearly wrong. Having stated that, the opposite is also true. Arrogant enterprise application vendors in the past would tell the client that if they wanted to benefit from their software solution they had better re-engineer their business accordingly. For smaller organisations this was the price paid for having designer-label software. And in fairness, it would be cheaper for them to re-engineer their processes than to pay for tailored software that met their current process engineering.

Whether it be users or suppliers in the driving seat, this spirit of non-cooperation is taking its toll at the process–IT interface and that is ultimately dampening the business value one should expect from the associated investment in IT.

Nobody knows business like IT

Users need to keep in mind that nobody knows a process like the person who wrote the software to support it. I once had the misfortune to produce a software product based on a then-new piece of UK legislation called the Child Support Act. Turning law into software required having to reduce verbose and vague text (aka law) into cold logic that covered every eventuality. This resulted in me understanding that piece of law, at the time, better than the lawmakers. I am not claiming to be a legal hotshot; it is just the process of producing software that requires the developer to become very intimate with the legislation or process being automated.

Better still, the IT department is unique, with perhaps the exception of finance, in that it sees the enterprise as a whole. The IT department is truly unique in that it also has an inter-process perspective. Admittedly the CEO should have this too, but not necessarily at the data flow level. This heady combination of intimate process knowledge coupled with expertise on the process-chains running through the business must surely make the IT department worth consulting in respect of IT and business matters?

Many organisations fail to recognise that they actually have an in-house business process consultancy that has genuine organisational expertise. That is a whole lot of IT value lying untapped. There are of course good reasons for this non-utilisation, which we will explore in the next section.

It's not always IT's fault

Industry and the public sector are littered with examples of how IT has let down the users. The poor manner in which the IT department generally engages the business has played no small part in many such failures. The IT department – through lack of voice, a poor understanding of public relations or through sheer exasperation – has failed to defend itself where the problem was conceived by the business. Once the IT department develops a reputation for not defending itself, it becomes an easy whipping boy when departmental heads are brought to account for failures in their parts of the business.

Would it really be reasonable to blame the telecoms provider for a failed telesales campaign? Of course it would if the phones did not work. But the supplier cannot be blamed for the output of untrained telesales staff using perfectly functioning phones. Similarly the IT department, having delivered a new customer relationship management system, cannot always be blamed for the lack of sales success. If the system repeatedly crashes then IT is squarely to blame, if the system performance requirements have not been implemented into the new system. Similarly, if the users cannot navigate software because of poor/no system training then IT is also to blame. But when the system is not being used because, whilst mapping beautifully onto the documented business processes, it does not work well with the actual business processes then the question of blame is less clear-cut.

Given the parlous state of many business processes, it is no surprise that any attempts by the IT department to support these processes will lead to weeping and a gnashing of teeth.

Compliance

I mentioned earlier that the onslaught of regulatory compliance is having a seismic effect on the IT department. Similarly, it is impacting business processes. Some organisations have recognised the degree of investment needed to become compliant. Other organisations treat compliance as simply another user application that, once written, can be lowered onto the existing infrastructure.

Compliance, like security, is not a "bolt-on". Compliance requires business surgery. Each process needs to be re-examined to establish whether "compliance controls" are to be added. This in turn will require a revisitation of the supporting software. Compliance offers the perfect excuse for a spot of business process re-engineering (BPR). A major overhaul of the processes is the perfect opportunity for the IT department to pull up the technology floorboards and overhaul the complete IT infrastructure.

The increasing security demands of the last few years should have prompted this exercise. But overhauling the IT infrastructure is a major exercise that will trigger phrases like "write off" and "poor investment" in the minds of business leaders. So only the bravest of CIOs would broach this subject. But compliance with its incarceration implications seems to elicit a more positive response from the executive team. This represents a window of opportunity that will not remain open for ever.

Entwinement

Like strategy, there appear to be three levels of enlightenment in respect of IT and processes:

- **Level 1.** The organisation, with reluctance, uses the IT department to automate the process for improved efficiency.
- **Level 2.** The organisation recognises the value of the IT department and so treats it as a very valuable supplier.
- **Level 3.** The organisation recognises the value of the IT department both as a supplier of process efficiency and as a business process adviser. Consequently, the organisation treats the IT department as a partner.

Level 1 represents a dysfunctional organisation that will in time wither and die. Alternatively, they may be acquired by an organisation that is astute in spotting level 1 organisations and resolving the associated business–IT conflicts. This relatively small repair exercise could dramatically increase the value of the acquired organisation. Venture capitalists, take note.

Level 2 organisations have managed to tame the IT department. The service levels are in place and the IT department is expected to deliver to those levels. The IT department is customer-sensitive but is not encouraged to participate in business-related decisions. Organisations that are at level 2 have managed to align their processes and IT.

Level 2 IT departments typically adopt a "just enough engineering" or "adequate is enough" policy. The aim is to meet the service level agreement (SLA) and nothing more. This mindset presumes that the users have sufficient wisdom in respect of IT to dictate the manner in which IT is used. This is less dire than level 1, but is still a cause for concern as the users are rarely well enough informed to optimise their use of IT, which will in turn lead to a relatively low return on the IT investment. An IT department that is operating in a "clipped wings" environment will be powerless to intervene. This will have a morale-sapping effect on the IT department as the associated problems of this unilateral relationship come to light.

Level 3 represents IT–process entwinement. The organisation recognises the IT department's ability to improve the efficiency of its processes. It also acknowledges that there is no point making processes more efficient if they are flawed processes. Level 3 organisations also acknowledge that new technologies can deliver competitive advantage and so it is essential to include the IT department in critical business decision-making.

Level 3 organisations are not afraid to take a cold look at their existing business processes, and business process flows, with a view to re-engineering them. The IT department will play a key role in maximising their effectiveness as well as their efficiency. It is likely that the new processes will be designed so that they can adapt easily to changing market conditions, and advances in new technologies.

Organisations that have become on-demand, agile, real-time and so on have recognised that process–IT entwinement is a fundamental precept. The IT department has an evangelical role to play in helping organisations understand the importance of process–IT entwinement. Once the message is sold, so to speak, the IT department needs to prepare itself to come out from behind the IT department sandbags and engage with the users in a business-focused manner. For many organisations this is a lofty ambition. But nothing less is required if sustainability is part of the strategic plan.

Rationale Summary

Information technology is key to automating business processes. Therefore, the extent to which the management of IT and processes is entwined will determine the quality of the processes, and therefore the success of the business. This layer of the IT Value Stack provides a great opportunity for the IT department to become business advisers.

As we will see in the next section, there are a number of reasons why process–IT entwinement does not happen in practice.

Process Entwinement – Why it Doesn't Happen

Information technology has the power to make business processes more efficient. It can also provide the golden thread that links processes together to enable different parts of the business to operate as an effective team. So why is the entwinement of processes and IT more a vision than a reality in many organisations? This section explores the obstacles blocking the path to process–IT entwinement.

Business knows best

Many organisations see the IT department as a subservient supplier that should obey instructions without question. The IT department has done itself no favours in this respect. Most high-profile project failures are the result of the IT department misinterpreting what the users actually needed. This has in turn driven many businesses to tighten the reins in respect of their relationship with the IT department.

But some businesses have become overzealous in their management of how the IT department serves the users. They go beyond simply demanding what they require, as in "We need a front office trading system" to specifying how they would like it implemented, as in "We want to use package X". Now package X may well be the most cost-effective option, but I feel this is overstepping the professional boundary. Much like telling your doctor what is wrong with you and then going on to explain to her the course of action she should advise you on.

In both examples above the "user" may well be right. They have consulted the web or spoken to someone with a similar problem. But technologists, unlike users, (should) have a better perspective on the implications of introducing new technologies into the existing infrastructure. Much like doctors can see the wider implications of a given treatment, taking into account the patient's medical history and actual symptoms.

Given the highly directorial nature of the relationship, it is unlikely that the technologists' views will be sought in respect of the business condition requiring "treatment". Sometimes the users are unwittingly asking for a system to automate a flawed process. The IT department, by unswervingly delivering the system, becomes responsible for enhancing the defectiveness of the business. So IT, and thus the IT department, gets the resultant blame. But there is nothing wrong with the technology, which now enables the process to be more efficiently flawed. But the IT department should have seen this coming and been more influential in the early stages of the engagement.

That is easier said than done, when the request for a new system is being made by the new CFO who is using this as an opportunity to let the CIO know who is the "alpha manager". Ostensibly it is a business request, in reality it is the CFO imposing their will on the IT department. Unfortunately, the CFO–CIO hierarchy is one of the most damaging obstacles to levering best value from one's IT investment.

Too tech-centric

The traditional role of the technologist is to develop and support IT systems. The nature of IT development, particularly in respect of large systems, led to many technologists having no idea as to what the system was supposed to do or what the business case was for building it. Out of hundreds, maybe thousands of modules that would make up the system, programmers would be given one or more modules to code. Being so technically involved in the innards of the system made understanding the complete system a luxury. Over time many technologists simply accepted that it was someone else's job to see the big picture and learnt to find meaning in their work despite being clueless about the business rationale for their involvement.

This cultural mindset permeates many IT departments today. The technologists are content to be technology-focused. The idea of engaging with the users and challenging their business processes is unthinkable, even if the users invited them to do so.

Perhaps surprisingly, I meet many people working in IT departments who want to engage with the users. But usually these are people employed as technologists who have since discovered they don't like technology (or possibly technologists). Getting closer to the users for them psychologically is like the prisoner who wants to spend more time near the prison walls. If nothing else it increases their chances of escaping. I will be pleased when I meet more people who enjoy technology and who also want to engage with the users. We are not there yet.

It's safer behind the sandbags

As a developer, the last thing I wanted was to hear from the users. As far as I could work out at the time, they were fickle people who seemed incapable of sticking to their guns in respect of their requirements. Much like the trepidation associated with an unwanted sales call, where you have a strong sensation that the caller does not necessarily have your interests at heart, a call from a user usually meant disruption to your work. Imagine being engrossed in the latter stages of a crossword puzzle and you are then instructed to abandon it and commence work on solving a different puzzle. This is both frustrating and dispiriting.

The fixed price paradigm has forced the users to get their requirements right first time and the IT department (or supplier) to deliver on that on time and within budget. This model was designed to help users constrain the level of spend on IT projects. Unfortunately, it has encouraged the IT department to close the shutters whilst they deliver, because changes to the requirements will result in more work without necessarily more allocated resources. This leads to IT departments minimising their contact with the users. Climbing over the sandbags and engaging with the users in respect of process design is not an attractive option if it is going to ultimately generate more work for the IT department. More work is not the problem (ask any empire-building CIO) but more work without extra resources to handle it is rarely appealing.

CIOs don't even see the value

I have worked in many organisations where the IT departments are larger than many significant IT service providers. The IT departments are servicing a number of business functions that each have a number of IT-related service offerings. What amazes me is how some of these businesses treat IT as a commodity. For example, project X will need N (where N is greater than one) "techies" this financial year. The product manager in charge of the service offering will then attend the annual auction where he will bid for his N techies. Much like livestock fairs (or perhaps even worse), there is no need to see the resumes of each "beast". As long as they display the broad characteristics one is looking for then they will do. The auction may descend into a bartering session, where those that are expert in trading IT bodies get what they want in terms of IT resource. The upshot of this is that technologists are allocated almost randomly to different projects each year.

The influence of the barterer being potentially greater than that of the strategic imperatives can result in your best IT people being sucked onto pet projects that are not entwined with the business strategy. This approach to "IT resource" allocation is unhealthy. From the technologists' perspective, they get a lot of variety as a result of this approach, which perhaps makes their world more interesting. But they never actually develop any expertise in a key business process. By the time they start to become expert in – say – back-office foreign exchange systems, they are shifted to private banking. So at the end of the day, the IT department doesn't have any genuine expertise in the business processes, because the staff are shuffled around almost randomly. Thus even the most seasoned technologists find themselves repeatedly in novice mode as they try to come to terms with the business context of their latest project.

The fact that CIOs allow their staff to be used in this manner suggests that they do not see the value in their staff building up genuine expertise in the business processes. Until this is addressed, the IT department will be unable to deliver business process advice, thus reducing the IT department to a "low value adding" body shop.

CIO bottleneck

Even where there is genuine in-house expertise, IT departments are typically not very good at selling their capability to the business. Often this is because the CIO cannot get the attention of senior executives, and so cannot pitch for the process-related business. Or even if they get "face time" with the CEO, they do not have the influencing skills to sell the idea. As a result, CIOs remain trapped in reactive mode; their job being to ensure that the service level commitments are kept, regardless of the flaws in some of the business processes.

Should the CEO actually buy the concept of "the IT department as process consultants", there need to be some changes to the IT budgeting model to permit the IT department to influence the business processes without being penalised. In other words, should the IT department identify business process improvements, which require changes to the supporting IT systems, it should be allocated the resources needed to deliver on this new requirement rather than be expected to steal resources from its existing commitments. This rarely happens.

Service-level agreements are excellent for promoting a mediocrity mindset, "do what is necessary, and not a jot more". The CIO needs to be more influential and promote this latent capability. It may well require nothing less than a sustained public relations campaign to reposition the IT department's capability in the eyes of the business. This requires business skills that are not currently seen as core to the role of CIO. And the CIO's staff similarly need to be equally influential if the IT department's process advisory service is to gain traction. This is an opportunity for the training department to play a significant role in unleashing the latent value buried in the IT department.

Cultural resistance

Even with an influential IT department that manages to sell the process adviser concept to the boardroom, there is still the issue of getting user buy-in. Users may have reason to obstruct the automation and/or enhancement of associated business processes. Potentially this may lead to their role becoming redundant and so they will perceive approaching technologists as the Grim Reaper.

Similarly, some staff are not overly keen to support the automation of processes because it may reduce the value of their "bargaining chips". Sales people come to mind. The more customer information they transcribe to the customer management system, the less personal control they have over that customer. Once institutionalised, other sales people can access that data. As a sales person, I would be loath to share data on a key relationship

I have nurtured for several years, if there is a real chance that my "colleagues" are going to harvest the relationship for short-term gain. This is bad for me as I have lost control of the relationship to my employer; a selfish, but common, perspective.

Automating the associated processes might well make logical sense, but that does not take into account the motivations of the users. In this case, working with HR might resolve the issue, particularly if I was remunerated for not just winning business but for sharing my knowledge. This is a detailed point, but it illustrates why so many CRM systems are sitting idle around the globe. Information technology staff need finely honed empathy and political skills to emerge from this engagement unscathed. Some users are actually very happy with the existing set of inefficient and even ineffective processes. Such changes need senior level sponsorship and perhaps even a programme in "DNA cleansing". Failure may be the alternative.

Unscrupulous vendors

Some vendors, particularly in a "large vendor, small buyer" scenario, can bully the buyer into taking their IT solution, knowing that for it to work will require a re-engineering of the buyer's business processes. Some small clients are nimble enough and happy enough to accept this as the price of designer-label software. Sadly, some are not and only discover this post-implementation. Invariably the IT department takes the heat, which is justified unless they were forced into this purchasing decision by a senior executive who happens to be a friend of the vendor's chairman.

Technology weakness

IT has the potential to truly improve business processes, not least by supporting their automation. Increasingly the IT industry is providing business intelligence tools that allow users to glean insights through analysing the associated process data. That aside, IT still has a long way to go in respect of its potential in supporting business processes. Why, for example, are the majority of business process intercommunications handled by something as unreliable and manually driven as email? And why have workflow and groupware solutions proved to be so elusive in practice? And by the way, where is the much-touted paperless office? There are various content and document management solutions out there, but many of these are a hybrid of paper and paperless solutions. Some will justifiably argue that cultural inertia is the obstacle. So perhaps if we give it a generation or two to mature, paper will become *passé*. Today paper exists and that undermines the automation of business processes. Paper is also costly, unecological and unsecure.

The death of staff

If we take the view that IT has the capability to automate practically all business processes and their intercommunication, then the majority of most businesses should be electronically seamless, with humans only involved by exception. Organisations will only need humans where a computer is less likely to perform the task as well as a human, for example, handling a customer complaint empathically, creating innovative customer solutions or in strategic planning. We are certainly not at this point yet, thanks to the problems highlighted above.

Problem Summary

The "end game" for process automation looks ugly for those that believe there is dignity in labour. In theory, the automation of essentially drudge-processes will free up many of us to pursue higher endeavours, most likely outside the confines of our employer, or even employment. There is certainly some way to go in respect of automation before the company server determines business strategy. But in the meantime many organisations that need to compete on the global playing field will need to address these process–IT entwinement issues if they want to remain competitive.

Towards Better Process Entwinement

The IT department has a lot to offer the business in respect of process advice. Both the IT department and the users need to recognise this. In this section we look at the steps that you can take to improve your process–IT entwinement.

Be clear on process definitions

This includes the critical process chains that run through the organisation. Processes fall into the following categories:

Undocumented. This can mean that there is no actual process and so each time this part of the business is triggered, the associated actions and maybe even the resultant outcomes are somewhat random. Sometimes the process delivers very predictable results, where there is no documentation, because the documentation resides in the heads of the associated users. This is less worrying than no documentation, but still represents a lack of control from a business perspective, and an unnecessarily high reliance on the staff. Undocumented processes in whatever form are dangerous territory for IT staff. This will need immediate attention. The corporate governance military police will view this in the same way as law enforcement agents view a major drugs bust.

Documented and not followed. This is the most soul-destroying from an IT perspective. The technologists build an elegant system to support the documented processes, but nobody uses the system because the documented processes have purely theoretical value. This is in some ways worse than undocumented processes because it instils a false sense of security in the IT staff tasked with automating these processes. Management attention is required because users who are happy to work in this manner are clearly out of control. Technologists should keep their distance until the land mines are cleared. Or, more proactively, offer to (re-)engineer the processes concerned.

Documented and followed. This is of course a much more healthy starting point, but it is only a starting point. Unless the documentation is heavily supported with diagrammatic techniques whereby all parties interpret the diagrammatic notation in the same way, there will be a lot of opportunity for misinterpretation. This is where it pays for IT staff to develop expertise in the business processes they contribute to. For a mortgage company, "default" means one thing to the IT department and something else to the customer. Technologists should presume nothing and double-check everything. Time would be well spent in creating a glossary of terms that all parties understand. Once everyone is on the same page, then the technologists are in a position to share their insights into how the process might be optimised. Technologists need to have both the confidence to sell their perspective, despite potential opposition, and also the humility to recognise that perhaps, on occasion, the users have a better perspective.

Engage with all stakeholders

Users are very sensitive to having new processes and systems imposed on them. Much like personal clothing, wearers want to control or at least influence the buying process. Therefore it would be folly to not seek their input. It might be tempting to let the process manager or even the business sponsor determine the requirements. They should have a more strategic view than process users. But it pays to consult real users, and to ensure they know why the change is taking place. Processes are only as good as their users' willingness to adhere to them. In business terms, nothing is worse than a user scorned.

Be aware of ex-users who see themselves as wise old owls that have great insights into the strengths and weaknesses of the given process. They may well have, though sometimes their knowledge is "suspended in amber" from a time when they were actual users. The reality is that the business has moved on and they are often oblivious to this fact.

So, to avoid being misdirected, involve all stakeholders, including customers and supplier as necessary. Avoid users at your peril. External suppliers of IT services take note of this. Often the sponsor may have an agenda that is not necessarily in the best interests of the users or the business (or you). Keep in mind that if either of those parties is unhappy, there will be repercussions. So insist, making it a condition of engagement if necessary, that exposure to all stakeholders is available when gathering process requirements.

Engineer the corporate DNA

In general, users and technologists need to reposition themselves in respect of their relation to IT and business. This will require skills acquisition, knowledge transfer and even an attitude shift. For some staff the attitude shift will be all too much. These people will need to be managed out of the organisation, freeing them to find an organisation with more traditional values in respect of process–IT entwinement.

The New Era user and IT staff profiles need to be fed into the recruitment process. This will stem the acquisition of "old-school" mindsets. In some cases old school thinking may be so ingrained that IT staff development will yield little gain and so replenishment of the gene pool via recruitment will be required. We will explore staff development in more detail below. In respect of processes, users will need to understand how to engage with the technologists such that misinterpretation of the requirements is minimised. They must also treat technologists as strategic partners rather than as subservient suppliers.

Crudely speaking, the end game requires that:

- All user-shy "propeller heads" are removed from the IT department.
  - Or at least corralled away from the business interface, if their technical capability remains valuable to the organisation despite their lack of business orientation.
- All IT staff develop genuine expertise in the business, specifically the areas of the business they support. Being good at technology is not enough.
- All user technophobes are removed from the business.

Incentivise action

Having re-engineered the workforce to be both IT-centric and process-sensitive, it is time to encourage these former combatants to engage. The adage "what can't be measured can't be managed" is appropriate here. All processes, or at least the business-critical ones for starters, need to be constantly measured, in much the same way as a sports centre will check that the swimming pool temperature lies within the recommended range, or that no "users" are trapped under a loaded barbell as a result of an over-ambitious bench press attempt.

This will be obvious to most people, but what to measure might require more thought. Fortunately, process management is relatively mature and approaches such as six-sigma are spreading like a religious cult. Six-sigma in particular has a strong focus on quality, i.e., the extent to which the process performs as planned. Pizza companies have relatively refined processes relating to delivery, as their customers in particular have a great interest in how the actual delivery time relates to that stated on the marketing literature. The associated penalties for late delivery act as a natural incentive.

Other measurements include:

Usability. How intuitive and ergonomic are the IT systems that support the process?

Security. How robust are the IT systems in respect of minimising inappropriate access?

Performance. To what extent do the IT systems perform at a level that is appropriate for the user? Languid trading systems can cost investment banks a lot of money.

Governance. How supportive are the IT systems in respect of management reporting?

If both users and technologists are given bonuses based on the extent to which the processes perform as expected, then it is likely that the processes will perform as expected – particularly if the bonus is a significant element of their remuneration. One hopes that incentives will improve staff behaviour. If the bonus is significant then it will also serve as a "stick" for those that do not see the health benefits of carrots, as it were – particularly if the absence of a bonus takes their remuneration into the "poverty zone". Whether both parties like each other or not, they will work out a way to put their differences aside if the incentives are wisely chosen. Service-minded technologists should welcome this approach. Users may be bemused by it, wondering why they are being rewarded for what is essentially the job of the IT department. This is likely to be an indicator of a disentwined mindset, and therefore an indicator of the need for some DNA re-engineering.

Scale down analysts

I have no axe to grind personally with business and systems analysts, but I do believe their existence protects users and technologists from direct engagement, which is exactly why they came into existence in the first place. It was appropriate then, it shouldn't be now. It is time for these go-betweens to disappear into the background and let the users and technologists progress what will hopefully be an intimate, and even entwined, relationship.

It would be unwise to purge all analysts from the organisation, because the road to process–IT enlightenment is a long one. Whilst it might seem counterintuitive, I think that business and systems analysts should start to think about becoming technologists. The technology tools are becoming less technical and more aligned to business processes (some older technologists might argue that IT stopped being technical with the demise of assembler programming). Analysts could potentially represent the new generation of hybrid business technologists, though I suspect many will not necessarily relish the thought of this. In any case, it would be a kindness to alert the analysts to the fact that they need to re-skill or become a casualty of war in the evolving information revolution.

Action Summary

Process–IT entwinement is critical to organisations getting best value from their IT investment. Unless the IT department is allowed to influence the engineering/re-engineering of processes, it is in danger of delivering working systems that impressively automate flawed processes – thus enabling the business to fail on a more impressive scale. The IT department then takes the heat when that becomes apparent. The business is encouraged to tease the technologists out from behind the sandbags so that they engage with the business. Harnessing the process wisdom residing in the IT department will be a source of competitive advantage for some time to come. If that does not compel you into action, there will come a point when process–IT entwinement becomes an entry condition to compete in your market, so you may as well address this sooner rather than later.

Process Entwinement – External Perspectives

This section provides an alternative view to my own in respect of process entwinement. The contributors were asked to answer one or more of the following questions:

- Why is process entwinement important?
- Why is this not generally being addressed?
- What are the underlying problems?
- What are the consequences of failing to address this issue?
- What advice would you give in respect of process entwinement?

Why is process entwinement important?

> "IT failures" are typically not technology related. This is often because businesses refuse to change their processes to benefit from the new technology.
>
> **Karen Mellor, IT Capability Associate Director, Astra Zeneca**

Many organisations do not realise the value their IT department can deliver to the business over and above the delivery of IT-driven services. The IT department touches every aspect of the business and so is in a strong position to advise on company wide matters.

Rob Fraser, IT Director, Alliance Boots

IT departments often base their designs on a formal requirements document that has been drafted in haste without reference to the "informal" processes that already exist due to process breakdowns or IT deficiencies. Often these documents are poorly validated and do not engage all the relevant stakeholders.

Ketan Varia, Business Process Consultant, kinetik solutions

Invariably it takes all parties to play their part in any IT project – setting up the hardware and software is clearly an IT function. Getting the processes to work correctly is as much a business responsibility as it is IT. IT should act as champions. Usually in a good application support team they may have as much experience as the users. But it is the users' (business) responsibility to sign off the application. They own the process not IT. IT are the mechanics not the drivers.

Vivian Ash, Group Information Manager, BASF

Process entwinement is critical because this is the point where the value from IT investments (i.e., projects) is realised. Fail at this point (i.e., to embed IT into the business and realise the anticipated business change) and the entire project investment is wasted.

Richard Boreham, IT Strategy, Governance and Performance
Practice Leader, KPMG

Businesses are processes – business efficiency is a product of process efficiency.

Nick Leake, Director of Operations and Infrastructure, ITV

Why is this not generally being addressed?

People have staff assigned to projects both within IT and business areas who are ill equipped to find a solution that really delivers the ROI.

Karen Mellor, IT Capability Associate Director, Astra Zeneca

It is much easier for IT to take up formal requirements or information from a senior manager. Often the solution is over engineered. Often the solution has no impact on the effectiveness of the "end to end" process.

This can be addressed by working with people at the "coal face" and understanding:

- Where the process issues are.
- What informal processes are in place
  - where formal process is not followed.
- Where IT can deliver sustained benefit.
- Where IT engineering becomes over-engineering, resulting in the creation of more issues then benefits.
  - For example, a complicated online form may make database analysis better (and may fit with the functional requirement) but drives the customer away or even worse forces the customer to accept default values in an attempt to quicken the process. A user-centric approach is required.

Ketan Varia, Business Process Consultant, kinetik solutions

The tools to easily understand, model and manage processes do not exist.

Nick Leake, Director of Operations and Infrastructure, ITV

What are the underlying problems?

In many instances:

- Staff don't follow a project management framework.
- The scope continually changes.
- Budget is not assigned to the project, but comes from a general pot which keeps being filled.
- The benefits of the project are not identified at project outset.

Karen Mellor, IT Capability Associate Director, Astra Zeneca

Usually a lack of ownership from the business. It is easier (and sometimes more sensible) to get IT to put the processes in. If it is badly implemented then it is obviously IT's fault. Wrong – it is IT's fault to get too deeply involved in a process without the business playing their part.

Vivian Ash, Group Information Manager, BASF

The underlying problems are the barriers that separate different functions (sometimes aided and abetted by IT).

Ketan Varia, Business Process Consultant, kinetik solutions

Process entwinement is difficult to realise for several reasons:

- Benefits realisation is difficult to track in comparison to other project metrics. For example, most project process centres around delivering a "product" (e.g., an implemented system). Benefits realisation takes a different viewpoint and continually challenges the rationale for the project.
- It is not just IT that is responsible. The business is equally responsible for exploitation. Consequently, the business needs to be as good at this change exploitation as (and probably better than) their "professional project advisors" in the IT function.
- Projects are now much better understood to be a combination of both IT delivery and business change workstreams. Unfortunately, the emphasis all too often remains on the "hard" delivery aspects of IT project delivery – and not equally on the "softer" re-engineering, change and training aspects that need to occur within the business.

- Finally, the IT function rarely has the skills or capability in its portfolio to help the business with these aspects of the project delivery. As a result, the IT function concentrates on the IT aspects of the project.

Richard Boreham, IT Strategy, Governance and
Performance Practice Leader, KPMG

What are the consequences of failing to address this issue?

The company lags behind, stifled of innovation leading to mediocre results.

Karen Mellor, IT Capability Associate Director, Astra Zeneca

Usually finger pointing over badly implemented systems – with each side accusing the other of not listening.

Vivian Ash, Group Information Manager, BASF

Very quickly after the euphoria of going live, new informal "work around" processes are created as the IT solution fails to satisfy either the users or the customers. Such informal processes then lead to subsequent IT solution failures. Consequently, users lose motivation and turnover of staff increases. Of equal concern is the associated degradation in the customer experience.

Ketan Varia, Business Process Consultant, kinetik solutions

Process inefficiency.

Nick Leake, Director of Operations and Infrastructure, ITV

What advice would you give in respect of addressing this issue?

Introduce the concept of the "change team". In order to maximise the value out of any IT delivery there needs to be a change team within the project that fully understands:

- The business.
- The project drivers.
- How to deliver value through IT.

Other recommendations include:

- Sort out the portfolio
  - Ensure a balance of creative high risk strategic projects alongside the necessary operational support projects.
- Tighten up governance, make rules and stick to them.
- No project sign-off unless real benefits are delivered.
- Conduct post-project reviews publicly to both business and IT groups.

Karen Mellor, IT Capability Associate Director,
Astra Zeneca

Organisations should capitalise on the process expertise lying dormant in their IT department. At Alliance Boots we have the challenge of managing an array of offerings that are both broad and deep. It is thus quite easy to introduce complexity into our processes. We thus place great focus on understanding and managing the "cost of complexity". Given our IT department's ability to advise on process issues, our executive team recognise the value in engaging the IT department at the core of this activity.

Rob Fraser, IT Director, Alliance Boots

This is a complex and intertwined area to address but it requires:

- A focus on building the capability equally across business and IT.
  - Customer side capability will also be valuable.
- The IT department to deliver the basics well and drive its own credibility through reliably delivering on its obligations (i.e., building the right systems).
- A decision by the organisation as to where it places its "process entwinement" capability.
  - It could be positioned in the project resource pool that lives in IT. Or it could be created within the business along with project management capabilities there. In this second case it is imperative that the participants have a professional project delivery ethos.

Richard Boreham, IT Strategy, Governance and Performance Practice Leader, KPMG

Identify the key processes that have to be optimised and concentrate on them.

This problem would be reduced if all parties had:

- A common language for process modelling.
- Common and easy to use tools.

There is also a need for process owners and executers (business staff/employees) to be able to set out their universe or total set of processes and model them.

Nick Leake, Director of Operations and Infrastructure, ITV

What other related points would you like to add?

Fundamentally, process entwinement is not about delivering the "newest"/"best" or optimal technological solution. It is about exploitation of what is currently available. Good exploitation of mediocre technology solutions is more effective than waiting for an improved, elegant solution. The former will also be cheaper.

Security issues and regulatory compliance are now placing an emphasis on ensuring both embedded IT processes (and controls) and the business activities (including issues such as spans of control and access rights) are linked and understood. These aspects are not specifically additional drivers in the context of IT strategy and design. However, they need attention and must not be ignored because of "other priorities". There is a danger that this can then be perceived as a conflicting demand when compared with, say, meeting business demands to "just deliver".

Richard Boreham, IT Strategy, Governance and
Performance Practice Leader, KPMG

This is hard!

Nick Leake, Director of Operations and Infrastructure, ITV

PEOPLE ENTWINEMENT

"Trust is the lubrication that makes it possible for organizations to work."

Warren Bennis, US Educator

In this chapter:

- The need for people entwinement.
- People entwinement – why it doesn't happen.
- Towards people entwinement.
- People entwinement – external perspectives.

value management

circulation management

service management

technology management

people entwinement

process entwinement

strategy entwinement

The Need for People Entwinement

People are an organisational burden, what with their aspirations, variable work ethic, environmental requirements and industrial tribunals. But until computers completely obviate the need for people, they remain an essential and expensive organisational asset. And as such they need to deliver a decent return on that investment. Full value from the IT investment will only be reaped once the stakeholders are tuned to act as IT value amplifiers rather than value dampeners. These stakeholders include suppliers, senior executives, users and technologists, amongst others.

Essentially, people need to communicate – particularly, though not exclusively, across the business–IT chasm. Alignment suggests that the IT people need to fall into line with the needs of the business people. I think the relationship needs to be more peer-based, with the communication flowing in both directions, hence the emphasis on entwinement.

This section makes the case for focusing on people entwinement as an approach to improving the value obtained from one's investment in IT.

The IT value chain

To fully understand the role of people in respect of IT value, we need to understand the concept of the IT value chain. This chain runs through all the people (and therefore departments) involved, either directly or indirectly, with IT. It starts with external technology suppliers and culminates with your customers. The following have a role to play in this value chain:

- External technology providers.
- Marketing agencies promoting technology providers.
- Prospective IT employees.
- Contract IT staff.

- IT recruitment agencies.
- Procurement staff.
- Internal IT recruiters.
- Internal IT training departments.
- The IT department.
- IT helpdesk.
- The boardroom.
- Users.
- The customers.

There may be more than one value chain (see Figure 5.1), but they always work their way through the IT department, users and ultimately to the customer. The chain may start with the boardroom, or even a regulatory body. Or perhaps with prospective IT employees who communicate with external recruitment agencies, which in turn liaise with the internal IT recruiters.

The IT value chain is not linked together by technology but by people; those involved communicate with those on either side of them in the chain. For example, the internal IT training function communicates with the external training provider and the IT staff (delegates). The IT helpdesk

Technology → IT → IT Department → Users → Customer
Vendor   Procurement

Candidate → Recruitment → HR → IT Dept. → Users → Customer
technologist   Agency

User → Help → IT Dept. → Technology
   Desk   Vendor

Technology → The → IT Department → Users → Customer
Vendor   Boardroom

Figure 5.1   Examples of IT value chain flows

communicates with the users and the IT department. These conversations are either value-amplifying or value-dampening. Helpdesk staff who approach the IT department to solve a user problem, but cannot understand the IT department's advice, are likely to confuse the users and thus reduce their capacity to lever IT to achieve their business objectives. Such a help-desk person is a value-dampener, though it could reasonably be argued that the IT department – or more specifically, the technologists involved – are the root value-dampeners because they could not articulate their advice in a manner that made sense to non-technical people.

Business leaders who are duped into over-buying external IT services are value-dampeners because they have paid more per unit value than neces-sary. Possibly the fact that the business executives made a strategic business decision without the involvement of the CIO will in itself lead to a corrosive dampening of value. A resentful CIO may be less motivated to make the relationship with the new supplier work. The new supplier may take an arrogant posture because it has a boardroom sponsor, leading to a collapse in constructive dialogue. Again, all value-dampening.

A procurement officer who simply focuses on cost and whose *raison d'être* appears to be to "beat up" the technology suppliers is doing the organisation no favours. Information technology recruiters who are playing buzzword bingo with job specifications and candidate résumés are similarly value-dampening.

The key people that make up your IT value chain need to understand the role that IT plays in helping your organisation maximise its return on the IT investment. Many of these key people are ultimately costing the organi-sation money because their inability to influence IT-related matters effectively leads to bad IT-related decisions. Examples include, technologists being placed on the wrong training course, users specifying their IT needs in a vague manner, technologists intimidating users through the use of technology jargon, boardroom executives who avoid making IT-related decisions or at the other extreme make uninformed IT decisions without taking advice from the CIO, who in turn is not skilled enough to influence the executive in question.

The IT value chain does not show up in organisational charts, and many people are unaware that they are key nodes/links on this chain. The organisations that look at their people from an IT value perspective will yield the greatest return from their investment in IT. And those that do it first will become market leaders; particularly if their offerings are underpinned by IT.

People are expensive

Technology people are expensive – the overall total cost of ownership of these IT assets is very high. This needs to change, and the market is conspiring to make that happen. Technology is becoming more sophisticated, as are the tools used to deliver the technology, which in effect "dumbs down" the art of system development. The move to self-healing computers is reducing the demand for support staff. There will come a time when IT people will need to be adding clear business as well as IT value to their organisation if their employment is to be justified.

Users are also expensive, therefore they need to be "sweated" for maximum return. Future users will be akin to fighter pilots. As sophisticated information pilots they will be using the myriad of information presented to them to make business decisions in real time. Thus users who are technophobic/techno-indifferent do not have a future in business.

A coherent and cohesive culture is good for business

On the basis that the age of leisure, where people do not need to work because technology is single-handedly fuelling the global economic engine, is some way off, we will need to consider how to optimise our people to maximise value. There appear to be at least two tribes in most organisations: regardless of the tribal fragmentation, there is usually a divide that runs unsurprisingly in line with the boundary of the IT department. Technologists and users seem to see each other as genetically different and thus seem to exist in parallel spiritual planes; much like cows and sheep co-existing in the same field. Whether it be cows and sheep, or users and technologists, they often do not see a need to cooperate. Sheep rarely jump to the defence of cows when the latter are being led to slaughter. If both parties communicated better they might realise that they share the same fate. Knowing this in advance, they might be able to do something about it.

Somehow or other these two groups need to morph into one. Again, if it was possible to communicate what plans the farmer had for their long-term well-being, the sheep and cows may well decide to cooperate to change their planned destiny. Similarly, users and technologists need to realise that they should act as a team as that is the only way to guarantee the survival of their organisation. Clearly, each individual needs to see a correlation between the fate of their organisation and their own fate. Maybe it is time to start blending the DNA so that the distinction between technologist and user becomes blurred. In any case, the entwinement of users and technologists needs urgent attention if better IT value is sought.

So is strong leadership

Without strong leadership it is unlikely that the organisation will gravitate towards its business objectives. Given that IT is so important to modern-day organisations, leadership now needs to embrace IT leadership, which for want of a universal definition might be described as the process of leading others to achieve results through the use of new technologies.

So who should take responsibility for IT leadership? Traditionally it is the CIO, but in any substantial IT department there will be a fairly steep hierarchy and so IT leadership needs to permeate through people like project managers, applications managers, the Chief Technology Officer, infrastructure managers and even team leaders. If IT leadership does not trickle down to the "factory floor" then it is unlikely that the organisation will reap the full benefit of its IT investment.

But should IT leadership be regarded as an issue solely for the IT department? Well, ultimately IT is a strategic investment and the boardroom – with its responsibility for good governance – needs to play an active role in ensuring that the associated spend is undertaken wisely. Thus it has a leadership role to play in respect of IT. As mentioned, IT is too important to be left (abdicated) to the IT department. To a lesser but not insignificant extent, all those with management responsibilities within the organisation need to influence IT spend and thus need to assume a position of IT leadership. Even users need to guide the IT department to achieving their objectives.

So, IT leadership is not the responsibility of just one person, it needs to be built into the corporate DNA on both sides of the business–IT fence.

Rationale Summary

People are a critical element in extracting maximum value from one's IT investment. The IT value chain highlights the importance of this. Thus, it is well worth investing in your people to ensure that they are tuned to be value-amplifiers rather than value-dampeners in respect of IT. The need for better people entwinement is clear, so read on to find out why this is failing to happen in many organisations today.

People Entwinement – Why it Doesn't Happen

Until organisations are fully automated, people will play a very significant role in the creation of business value through the use of IT. Entwinement of IT and business people – i.e., how they communicate and cooperate across the user–IT department chasm – is required to ensure the value chain has no weak links. A strong chain will lead to amplified business value. But it would seem that the concept of the IT value chain (introduced in the previous section) is unknown to many organisations. The majority of people, through a lack of poor IT leadership, are indifferent – and in some cases hostile – to cultivating a relationship with those that sit across the "divide". Remarkably, the majority of technologists and users do not recognise that this poor communication is costing their employer money, which in turn may impact their employment prospects.

This section investigates why people entwinement is a widespread problem.

DNA profiling

Today the IT value chain is made up of people and technology, either being sources of value amplification or dampening. The people involved in the chain can be classified into three broad groups, namely (see Table 5.1):

Table 5.1 Corporate profiling

	Techno-aware	Business-aware	High IQ	High EQ
Technologist	Yes	Variable	Yes	No
Non-technologist	No	Yes	Variable	Yes
Para-technologist	No	Yes	Variable	Yes

- **Technologists** – e.g., technical architects, analyst programmers.
  - Understand technology, but they are often "a mile deep and an inch wide" in their knowledge.
  - Have a variable interest in business.
  - Have a relatively high IQ.
  - Have a relatively low EQ.
    - Emotional intelligence – interpersonal skills such as empathy and the ability to recognise that it is often better to be smart than right.
- **Non-technologists** – e.g., users, senior executives.
  - Do not understand technology.
  - Interested in business.
  - Have no interest in IT.
  - Have a variable IQ.
  - Have a relatively high EQ.
- **Para-technologists** – e.g., IT recruiters, IT trainers.
  - Do not understand technology.
  - Interested in business.
  - Have a variable interest in IT.
  - Have a variable IQ.
  - Have a high EQ.

These are of course generalisations, and exceptions occur at either end of the associated Bell curves. Technologists and non-technologists are well understood, and often easily identifiable. Para-technologists are perhaps less well known – they work as internal service providers to the IT department. To do their job effectively, they need to have a greater understanding of IT than users. An IT recruiter that does not understand the IT roles they are resourcing is likely to soak up company resources in wild goose chases and ineffective filtering of candidates. Similarly, an IT training department consultant that does not understand IT is unlikely to add value when technologists seek advice on skills development. Technologists, recognising that the IT training department is simply acting as a buzzword training broker, are likely to bypass the para-technologists and source their own training courses.

These three profiles also exist in supplier organisations such as outsourcers. Given that IT is core business, their non-technologists should hopefully have some interest in new technologies. Their sales staff, particularly those that are taking a consultative approach to selling, might be considered para-technologists – though this is typically more an aspiration than reality. In a perfect world, those involved in the IT value chain would perform like a highly trained team with a collective sense of destiny. But today this is fantasy. The communications between people on the IT value chain are nothing short of dysfunctional. Whatever the reasons behind this, the reality is that the existing state of affairs could not be less ideally suited to yielding maximum business value through IT.

So, let's take a look at some of the problems that are obstructing the path to people entwinement.

Speak different languages

To non-technologists, technologists seem to speak a foreign language. Actually, given the rate at which the marketing departments of technology vendors are spewing out new TLAs (Three Letter Acronyms), it is common for even technologists to be confused when they talk to each other. In any case many non-technologists, tasked with influencing IT-related business decisions, find themselves sitting in meetings where they have no idea what is being discussed. Some technologists regard this as highly amusing.

The "glazing over of eyes" seems to be a condition triggered in non-technologists when the subject of IT comes up. As IT becomes more central to business, there is a danger that non-technologists could develop permanently glazed eyes. Conversely, terms such as profit, loss, business lunch, balance sheet, sales and marketing are used only in the most enlightened technologist circles. The differences in language highlight the differences in perspective between these two communities. Para-technologists tend to gravitate towards the language of the non-technologists.

This language polarisation results in poor communication, which is the source of many business–IT-related problems.

Distrust abounds

Without doubt, poor communication leads to distrust. Those who do not share our life philosophies can similarly induce distrust. Technologists and non-technologists, as we have seen above, are different. Non-technologists struggle to understand why technologists love their seemingly boring jobs, and why their hobbies are essentially the same as their day job (for example, the "open source" cult). Conversely, technologists are amazed that the key driver for many users is "return on labour" – i.e., how to get paid as much as possible for doing as little as possible. Creating a common *esprit de corps* across both parties is going to be very difficult, given the philosophical differences. The IT industry has done little to position technologists as reliable deliverers of business value. The number of well-documented expensive IT failures has conditioned many users to view the promises of technologists with scepticism.

The relationship between para-technologists and technologists is generally underpinned by distrust. Take this scenario: you want to sell your house and so approach an estate agent. You inform the agent that you would like to sell your detached house. The estate agent asks you what "detached" means? This person, who is on the verge of "managing" one of your biggest personal financial transactions, does not understand real-estate basics. This should be a cause for concern. Similarly, learning and development professionals or IT recruiters who do not understand the language, issues and trends associated with the IT industry are likely to generate high levels of distrust amongst those that deal with them along the IT value chain. Distrust is a sure-fire value-dampener and so needs to be eliminated.

Lack of competence

Given that one cannot replace the existing antagonistic tribes overnight with universal hybrid business technologists fine-tuned to handle both business and technology matters, it will be necessary to consider enhancing your existing human capital investment. Ultimately, people entwinement requires people to have interpersonal skills. As mentioned, these do not come as standard with technologists. Again this is a gross generalisation, but sadly it reflects the industry norm. There are of course very skilled people influencers on the IT department side of the fence, often to be found within supplier organisations. The fact that their employers are paying a premium for such people suggests that this profile is still quite rare.

Non-technical people are increasingly required to influence IT matters, though many struggle with this. If, for example, the user cannot articulate their requirements in a technologist-friendly manner, then they should not be surprised if the associated delivery is not quite what they had in mind; technologists are not telepathic. Similarly, a lack of technology understanding will make users less able to appreciate the IT department's business-enhancing technology recommendations. So understanding IT will become increasingly important as more organisations become IT-centric in their approach.

Technologists with poor communications skills and users with poor understanding of what IT can do for their business will eventually be perceived as liabilities rather than assets in the eyes of their employers. In an IT-centric world, such people will have limited employment options.

Board to tears

The general absence of IT representation at board level is a cause for concern, given how important IT is to the organisation and given the level of associated spend. There are a number of reasons for this, including the fact that many senior executives have a low opinion of their CIO. They perceive the CIO as simply another techie, albeit an older one, who is more preoccupied with technology than with the business objectives.

Many boardrooms see IT as something that should remain confined to the IT department. By compartmentalising IT, the senior executives feel that they are in control, and this enables them to treat the IT department and IT in general as a "black box". Whether by design or by default, by doing this they are taking the view that IT is either non-strategic or simply a one-dimensional business function that does not impinge on other aspects of the organisation. The approach is similar to that used with the catering function, where only in extreme cases will the workings of the canteen have strategic implications. Applying this model to one's IT investment is flawed, given the role of IT in practically every aspect of business, both operational and strategic. In any case, the model is common and consequently senior executives have made no effort to understand what IT can do for their business.

This demotivates IT people, who thus see themselves as ancillary to the core business. Good IT people will gravitate to where their skills are valued, and even to where they might have a chance of enjoying genuine career progression. The boardroom's indifference to IT represents mismanagement of the organisation's assets. Shareholders will take a dim view of this, as will regulatory bodies. Today this is, sadly, a common problem.

People are expensive

Technology people are expensive. Labour costs are a major contributor to the high costs associated with IT ownership. There is a general market pressure to drive down the total cost of ownership associated with one's IT investment. In response to this, technology is becoming more self-healing, thus minimising the need for human babysitting. Similarly, the tools used to develop software are becoming more sophisticated, resulting in system development becoming less of an (expensive) art and more of a procedural process. There will come a time when IT people will need to be adding business as well as IT value to their organisation if their employment is to be justified. The problem today is that this transition is not happening fast enough.

Users are also expensive, therefore they need to be "sweated" for maximum return. Future users will be akin to fighter pilots. They can be considered as sophisticated business pilots, using the myriad of information presented to them in real time to make business decisions. Bringing this back to the mundane, tomorrow's retail bank counter staff will become highly sophisticated sales consultants. Should a customer venture into a bank, the employee will be able to see his financial profile, and make accurate product recommendations based on this profile. Users who are technophobic/techno-indifferent do not have a future in business. The problem is that we need this future today.

Both technologists and users need to justify their existence if they are to remain relevant in the IT value chain. Ironically, the end game for the IT industry is to eliminate technologists. Eating one's offspring, so to speak, cannot be good for one's state of mind. Perhaps this is nature's way of eliminating certain species that do not fit in with nature's plans. Possibly I am reading too much into this. Technologists need to adapt to the changing world, and they are currently not adapting fast enough.

IT leadership

The issue of IT representation at board level was mentioned earlier. Focusing on leadership within the IT department, we typically find that the closer the CIO resembles a technologist the more likely that he will truly lead the technologists. Watching technologists interact with each other is similar to watching a nature programme. The alpha male/female displays dominant traits, which while not usually physical, involve asserting their technical superiority. Most of the younger members of the technology pack try to mimic the leader, and ingratiate themselves when the opportunity arises. Some of the pack may make a bid for technology leadership by questioning a design decision. This is a high-risk strategy, but if successful will eventually result in a change of leadership. The official management generally has no control of this behaviour, and so managing technologists is truly like herding cats.

The macho nature of technology leads to dysfunctional teams. The team leader is more interested in asserting their dominance technologically than harnessing the expertise of the team to achieve business results. This is a cultural problem. Within the IT department, dominance needs to be replaced with leadership. It would appear that organisations value "technology smarts" more than leadership skills in their technology managers. Thus, many IT teams perform suboptimally.

Problem Summary

The problems in the main are fundamental. Skills and knowledge alone will not be enough. A cultural upheaval is required, and this takes time. A transfusion of "right stuff" DNA may be required if the existing attitudes are too deeply ingrained into the organisation. My main concern is that many organisations do not realise they have a problem. Downward pressure on pricing from empowered customers and globalisation, amongst other factors, will eventually drive this issue to the top of the boardroom agenda. Like some diseases, where the symptoms only manifest themselves in the latter stages, some organisations will realise what they have to do, but will have run out of time to take action.

One might ask why HR departments have allowed this to happen. The HR department is the most critical department in respect of fixing the IT value chain. Unfortunately, in most cases HR represents one of the nodes on the chain that is most in need of fixing. This is a major obstacle, and it needs to be addressed at the highest levels within the organisation.

Towards People Entwinement

People will ultimately determine whether your IT investment yields business value. As previously mentioned, there are some fundamental cultural differences between technologists and non-technologists. As previously alluded to, the ideal approach would be to make everyone redundant and start again with people who have the "right attitude". The world is not ideal, and employment law is not always written with the survivability of businesses in mind, so a less revolutionary approach is required. This section explores what can be done to entwine business and IT department staff such that they work together to make new technologies deliver business results.

The following actions are recommended to migrate your people to a more IT-centric culture. In other words, a culture that can generate maximum business value from your IT investment.

Revise the recruitment approach

Do not let people join your organisation unless they understand the importance of people entwinement and the role of IT in achieving business objectives. This applies to both technologists and non-technologists. Certain sectors, such as investment banking, already insist on their technologists being business-oriented from day one. On the user side I notice that those earmarked for the boardroom are often very IT-centric in their outlook. They recognise the increasing role IT has to play in business success. Rather than just letting the smarter staff work it out for themselves, ensure everyone who joins the payroll understands this. The upward pressure of IT-centricity will play a role in accelerating the culture change. It will also grow the gene pool for your organisation's future leadership.

Job number one in this respect will be to ensure that your HR function in general, and your recruitment function in particular, understand that IT staff need to be business-focused and non-IT staff need to be more IT-focused.

Bolster learning and development function

Your staff on either side of the business–IT divide represent a substantial investment. These assets need continuous nurturing, particularly as the business waxes and wanes in response to market changes. Perhaps the only predictable change is that business will become tougher and that IT will become critical to keeping businesses competitive. Thus, the training/ leaning and development (L&D) department has a critical role to play in IT value optimisation. Therefore, the L&D staff themselves will need to become sufficiently competent to take the lead in what will be a major change management programme.

Leaning and development departments are starting to come to terms with the fact that their role is not to be subject matter experts, but to be learning and development experts who lever the expertise of external suppliers to achieve the organisation's people development objectives. They also need to recognise that training, for example, cannot be classified as either technology- or non-technology-focused. Business courses need to embrace IT and vice versa for technology courses.

Job number one in respect of staff development will be to ensure that the L&D team are sufficiently developed to offer real value in these changing times.

Build trust

New technologies have changed the business world in the main for the better. There have been massive improvements in business productivity since computer usage evolved from "one per building" to "one per desk". Wireless technologies have untethered the workforce from their desks, enabling staff to get closer to their markets. So, given the amazing contribution the IT department has made to business progress, why is it still regarded with suspicion?

The IT industry is in its infancy and like some children it tries to do adult things in a clumsy and often unsuccessful manner. Over-ambitious grand design projects are just an example of where the IT department sabotages its own reputation. One day, successful mega-projects will be the norm. Today, the technologies are not up to it and nor are the approaches employed.

The IT department needs to launch a trust-building offensive. Step one would be to stop embarking on grand projects and stick to more modest endeavours, and thus develop a track record for success and consequently service reliability. Step two is to launch a charm offensive. For example, hold open days for the users where they can come into the IT department and marvel at the (carefully crafted) demonstrations of what IT can do for the business. Having got the attention of the users, take the opportunity to educate them on the issues associated with system development. Most importantly, educate the users on the importance of their role in delivering successful IT services.

Information technology departments are encouraged to behave like ethnic cuisine restaurants. In the restaurant the language used by the staff is that of the diners, and not the language used in the kitchen. Some diners develop greater trust in the restaurant if they are given a tour of the kitchen. To take the analogy further, diners unfamiliar with the cuisine appreciate staff recommendations. And all diners respond positively to attentive restaurant owners. Chief information officers take note.

Upgrade the board

The senior executives, whether they like it or not, are role models for the business, or at least the user side of the business. If they act in a techno-indifferent/technophobic manner then that will become the default behaviour of the organisation. A lack of IT representation at board level will ensure that those strategic decisions underpinned by IT – i.e., all decisions – will be made without full consideration of the options and issues. This constitutes poor governance, and ultimately poor performance.

So, invite the CIO onto the board. Your existing one may be more "grown up techie" than business executive. Decide quickly whether to put the incumbent through an intense boardroom tenderisation programme or replace him with a boardroom-ready model. The first job for the new arrival is to ensure that their boardroom colleagues are all brought up to a base level of competence in respect of IT. I am not referring to business executives writing and reading their own emails, though this should be encouraged, but coaching the executives to understand IT terminology, the issues and opportunities associated with IT, and the impact IT can have on their organisation. The CIO should see herself as the digital coach to the boardroom.

The CEO should encourage the CIO to work closely with the CFO and HRD. The former because of IT's important role in improving the bottom line, and the latter because it will be people that make this happen. The CFO might have a problem with the CIO as a peer rather than as a subordinate. By changing the hierarchy, the CEO is signalling that IT is more than just a tool for cutting costs. The move will also signal that the CEO sees the IT department staff as core talent and not merely non-strategic ancillary workers/commodities. Over time, within such organisations, the IT staff will be able to plot a path from where they are to becoming the CEO.

Encourage entwined culture

Encourage users and technologists to work together by entwining their destiny. Information technology staff who support the front-office traders might share in the traders' commissions. This will force the traders to squeeze IT harder, as they are now on the "traders' payroll". The technologists will, if they are of the right mindset, be only too happy to provide the traders with tools that will ensure even greater financial success for all concerned. This will create virtuous pressure within the IT department. The smart technologists will follow the money and push to support those areas of the business that will improve their financial condition. Everyone wins.

Drive out geeks and technophobes

These cultural extremes are bad for business. Geeks have a certain puritan nobility, their belief in technology for technology's sake is attractive to impressionable young technologists. Similarly, users who wear their IT ignorance as a badge of honour, a mark of their well-rounded personalities, are equally attractive to impressionable users who are concerned that becoming too *au fait* with IT will possibly lead to personality disorders or potentially render them less attractive to the opposite sex.

Such extreme characters are bad for business and need to be rooted out, as they set the cultural code. If they are business-critical do not leave them alone with younger members of staff.

Improve soft skills

Technologists need to build up their EQ (emotional quotient) levels. Being right is not always the same as being smart. Take this example of a male technologist who is attending a social function one evening. His partner, having just put on her new dress, joyfully asks how she looks. The technologist gives this due consideration. Having analysed the question and the answer, he responds to the effect that when one considers the standard set by today's supermodels his partner deserves a score of six out of ten. This may well be accurate but it is certainly not a smart thing to say.

Technologists need softer skills if they are going to venture beyond the black and white world of digital technology and engage with non-digital organisms such as people. The fact that people come in "shades of grey" discourages many technologists from engaging with users.

Improve business skills

Technology is being "dumbed down" and so technology skills will become commoditised. Smart technologists are starting to build up application-specific skills. Very smart technologists are using terms like TCO, ROI and Enron to get the attention of their senior business colleagues. Technologists are to be encouraged to become more aware of business, in particular why IT is critical to business success.

Improve IT skills

Users need to develop a better understanding of IT. Technologists are generally "a mile deep and an inch wide" in their knowledge. Business staff are encouraged to be "a mile wide and an inch deep" in their understanding. An inch deep is enough to be credible when speaking to technologists. A mile wide gives users an edge over their potentially "narrow minded" colleagues.

Overhaul IT management

As mentioned in the previous section, management within many IT departments is dysfunctional because of the competitive nature of technologists. This will require the equivalent of a spinal transplant. The new breed of management will have a good understanding of IT in general and a very good understanding of what makes people tick. Specifically, they will be skilled in achieving results through technologists.

Eliminate the DMZ

This demilitarised zone sits between the IT department and the business. Business and systems analysts roam backwards and forwards across the DMZ relaying messages to and from both tribes. This zone was created to stop users and technologists coming into direct and sometimes violent contact. This zone is actually an IT value roadblock, and it needs to go.

The way to remove it is to remove the analysts. Like the United Nations military they are not intended as a permanent solution. However, the zone should only be closed once the users and technologists have evolved to a level where they recognise each other as being on the same side.

Eliminate the IT department

The job will be done when the IT department no longer exists as a geographic entity. The technologists, who will in every respect look and behave like users, will sit in amongst the users. The "pure play" technologist is dead. The hybrid business technologist is, in my view, the template for the future.

In the future, the users will sound more confident when talking about IT matters. Conversely, the technologists will sound less like technologists when discussing IT matters. This is the nirvana scenario for business–IT relations.

Action Summary

There is a lot that can be done to entwine your people in respect of maximising IT value. What has to be done is quite simple, but it certainly will not be easy. A cultural tectonic shift is required. Early movers will gain competitive advantage. Late movers need to be careful they do not leave it too late, or they will follow the path of the dinosaurs, and become an historical curiosity/MBA case study.

People Entwinement – External Perspectives

This section provides an alternative view to my own in respect of people entwinement. The contributors were asked to answer one or more of the following questions:

- Why is people entwinement important?
- Why is this not generally being addressed?
- What are the underlying problems?
- What are the consequences of failing to address this issue?
- What advice would you give in respect of people entwinement?

Why is people entwinement important?

Technology success is about people. Without the right skills and the effective leadership of IT-enabled change, the best technology in the world will not reach its full potential.

Different people have different technology-related skills needs. For example, business managers and leaders need to understand how technology can help to deliver business objectives. Then there is the general workforce: employees who use technology in their everyday jobs and need IT user skills at increasingly sophisticated levels.

Then there are the IT professionals who develop, implement and manage the company's technology systems.

There is a trend towards the outsourcing of IT functions. As a result, businesses are increasingly looking for in-house IT professionals whose skills complement and build on those moved outside the company. Companies need business-oriented IT professionals who can work at the very heart of the organisation. They need IT professionals who can function in customer-facing roles and are prepared for and comfortable with ongoing change.

All this requires a sophisticated set of skills and understanding; one that encompasses business, communication, team working and project management skills as well as up-to-date technical knowledge. Increasingly IT professionals need to be able to translate business objectives into technology solutions, manage budgets and supplier relationships and work within virtual teams that transcend functional, geographical, cultural and linguistic boundaries.

Karen Price, OBE, CEO of e-skills UK

It's important because IT people think they know what business users want better than business users. More importantly they think they know without asking. They use a different language and don't understand the business in many instances. The divide between business and IT is getting narrower as efforts are made to understand "needs" more. In the pharmaceutical industry an IT group lacking an understanding of science is not going to gain the credibility of the business group.

Karen Mellor, IT Capability Associate Director, Astra Zeneca

Today, boards are charged with playing a pivotal role in overseeing corporate operations, implementing strategy and upholding the highest ethical standards. When fulfilling these responsibilities, boards rely heavily on technology solutions that connect silos of data and place information in the hands of those who need it most.

Yet, not all boards possess the technology expertise necessary to use new technologies to create innovative solutions and increase business efficiency. CIOs who have both technology and business know-how are generally confined to the e-suite. As a result, technology remains an enabler not a driver of business.

Heidi Sinclair, CEO Europe, Burson-Marsteller

The 21st century business world is highly competitive with unending pressure for increased efficiency and enhanced returns to the shareholder. The competition from India, China and other Asian economies is fierce and businesses are under enormous pressure to do more and more for less money in order to compete. Most enlightened businesses have realised that business and IT people in their organisation need to work in more closely aligned inter-disciplinary teams, and to this end are generally recruiting less technical Computer Science graduates and more graduates with rounded IT with business, language or management credentials.

Steve Tyler, UK Programmes Director, LogicaCMG

It is the same theme as strategy entwinement. We have all seen the consequences of not doing this. So rather than blaming "the system" or getting enraged with the IT department's delivery record, do something different and do it together.

Philip Wright, Corporate Services Director,
Standard Life Healthcare

Technologists have to understand business needs to be able to satisfy them.

Nick Leake, Director of Operations and Infrastructure, ITV

Why is this not generally being addressed?

I think it is now being addressed. Most businesses are recognising, for example, that it is cheaper to manufacture goods and undertake software development and support in lower cost locations. This means retraining of staff whose traditional job has now gone off shore in broader skills. For IT staff this will mean the development of personal, management and business skills.

Steve Tyler, UK Programmes Director, LogicaCMG

Many organisations are looking to address this issue. A first step is often to bridge the primary point of relationship between IT and the business. Setting up the "account interface" with credible senior IT managers who do understand the customer's needs and priorities is a good starting point.

Richard Boreham, IT Strategy, Governance and Performance Practice Leader, KPMG

People don't like change.

Nick Leake, Director of Operations and Infrastructure, ITV

What are the underlying problems?

Technologists definitely do not speak English! I guess the IT industry has grown up liberally using acronyms since its birth. Gradually this will change as universities offer more diverse technology oriented courses (e.g., IT with Business Studies) and arm graduates with more non-technology training (presentation skills, etc.) as part of the syllabus.

Steve Tyler, UK Programmes Director, LogicaCMG

- IT remains a specialist technical discipline that is seen as uncomfortably distant from mainstream business operations.
- Overall performance, or perception of that performance, of IT (e.g., in project delivery or service delivery) drags down the perception of IT and degrades the working relationships.
- IT does not make its own case (its performance, challenges and business responsibilities) well enough.
- Business managers do not themselves have an appreciation of IT. This remains a blank spot for many and one which applied to other disciplines (e.g., finance) would not be generally accepted.

Richard Boreham, IT Strategy, Governance and Performance Practice Leader, KPMG

- A lack of a common language.
- IT people talking of "the business" as if they are a separate race let alone in the same company.
- Business people failing to understand how a system needs to be managed and controlled.

Philip Wright, Corporate Services Director, Standard Life Healthcare

IT and business fail for one and one underlining reason alone – the lack of real positive bilateral communication. IT and the business at large rap themselves up with finger pointing viewpoints. At the core of any IT and business disconnection a broken communication problem exists that for the most part neither party have been willing to address thus far.

If addressed then real alignment would deliver revolutionary value, this is not technological issue. SOA and other new so-called technologies could not of themselves deliver value unless they were aligned and measured against true business need, needs driven by understanding of business problems.

Shaun Fothergill, EMEA Security and IT Strategist, CA

What are the consequences of failing to address this issue?

Poor technology adoption.

Nick Leake, Director of Operations and Infrastructure, ITV

What advice would you give in respect of addressing this issue?

Investment in technology is wasted if it doesn't meet business needs, its introduction isn't managed properly, and if people don't know how to use it. The key issue here is skills.

The role of IT professionals is changing beyond recognition. Businesses need to support continuing professional development for the IT workforce so that it can keep up with the ever accelerating pace of technological change and respond to changing business needs.

IT users need skills at increasingly advanced levels. Structured training that is flexible and can be tailored to the needs of the business and individual job requirements will often provide the best return on investment for employers. Ideally, such training leads to a recognised qualification while focusing on the skills people actually need to perform their job.

Employers also need to ensure that all managers and leaders across an organisation have the skills to manage IT-enabled change and get the best out of technology for their business areas.

In the UK, through Sector Skills Councils, such as e-skills UK, employers also have an unprecedented opportunity to influence and define the content of external qualifications and training – ensuring that the skills they need are the skills they get.

Karen Price, OBE, CEO of e-skills UK

Again there are many strategies for addressing these issues:

- Foremost is for IT to concentrate upon and deliver on its promises for service quality and project delivery. It must be a credible part of the organisation.
- Organisational design needs to be considered. IT as a centralised shared service can create too much organisational distance with business units. There are remedies such as placing more control for IT within the customer business units.
- Project members from both the IT department and user community need to be collocated, where possible.

- Care in constructing the IT supply chain. Many IT organisations use offshore or remote systems development. From the above point it should be clear that there still needs to be a high level of contact between all project members. This needs to be designed in when determining the sourcing strategy.
- IT does itself need to build bridges through involvements with the business. Training secondments and other opportunities for cross working are important.
- Longer-term career development is also an approach (development of hybrid managers). This does not mean that all managers should be generalists. However, managers are to be encouraged to take "out of box" assignments from time to time.

Richard Boreham, IT Strategy, Governance and
Performance Practice Leader, KPMG

- Get the people working together.
- Identify places where technologists can add value.
- Build good relationships between technologists and technology users.

Nick Leake, Director of Operations and Infrastructure, ITV

If the IT–business communication issue is addressed then the subsequent alignment would deliver revolutionary value. This is not a technological issue. New technologies cannot of themselves deliver value unless they are aligned and measured against true business needs. Such needs require the IT department to have a sound understanding of business problems.

Shaun Fothergill, EMEA Security and IT Strategist, CA

The CIO is a key person in respect of business–IT entwinement. His ability to influence the boardroom will be critical if the organisation is ultimately going to reap the full benefit of the IT investment.

Dr Robina Chatham, Visiting Fellow at Cranfield School of Management, provides a valuable perspective on the fact that many CIOs lack political influence at board level:

CIO lacks influence

The missing ingredient – political acumen

Ask any IT professional what words and phrases spring to mind when you mention the words "organisational politics" and nine times out of ten you will get responses such as:

- Doing deals.
- Scoring points.
- Personal agendas.
- Getting one over on one's colleagues.
- Secrecy and subterfuge.
- Mafiosi tactics.
- Win–lose.

But like it or not, organisational politics is a part of corporate life. Organisations, being made up of people, are essentially political institutions. All leaders have to deal with organisational politics but some are better at it than others.

The "political game" is not like chess (a game which many IT people are good at, incidentally). Chess is rational, logical and absolutely competitive. But because some CIOs interpret the "political game" as though it were like chess, they bring to organisational politics some dangerous assumptions. Amongst them, the most dangerous assumption is that organisational politics is competitive in the same way that chess is competitive:

- There are only two sides.
- There are a number of well-rehearsed and proven strategies.
- You should never reveal your strategy to your opponent.
- The purpose of the game is to beat the opposition (or they will beat you).
- Whatever you do to enhance your own position naturally weakens that of your opponent.
- Cool, logical, clever, unemotional people are best at the game.

For some CIOs, many of whom cannot bear to lose, the preferred option is not to play for fear of losing a game whose strategies they do not understand.

But none of these features of games like chess apply to organisational politics – except in dysfunctional organisations. Many very successful "players" of organisational politics are successful because they know that, unlike chess:

- There are many "sides" – or shades of opinion.
- Nothing is well-rehearsed or proven at the leading edge of organisational change.
- You should always discuss and share your views with those who may see things differently.
- The purpose of the game is for everyone to win.
- Enhancing your own position may also enhance the positions of others.
- Cool, logical, clever, unemotional people are often worst at the game; the political game requires intuition and feeling as well as knowledge and logic.
- It is about building relationships so that people will want to deal with you again.

Organisational politics is an art rather than a science; an art which many IT professionals are ill equipped to succeed at. I write from experience; my own background is indeed scientific; I was taught to think logically and rationally, to seek out the right answer or universal truth through empirical evidence and logical reasoning. As I progressed through the ranks of the IT profession I was sent on numerous "technical" courses; my man-management skills had however to be learned on the job, from watching and emulating those around me, i.e., my IT peers and boss! Now that I am a lecturer for a business school I often see IT leaders shrink away from the leadership courses we run saying that they are not for them and that IT management is "different" from general management and therefore the skills do not apply or are not relevant.

In my teaching I use a very simple formula for political success:

- Acting from an informed and streetwise position.
- Acting with integrity.

I use these two dimensions to construct the model below and illustrate each profile with animal analogies to create my political zoo. The *innocent sheep* acts with integrity, but hasn't a clue about what is going on in the organisational sense. The *clever fox* knows precisely what is going on but uses this knowledge to exploit the weaknesses of others. The *inept baboon* neither acts with integrity nor knows what is going on. The *wise dolphin* represents my icon of political success.

Sheep	Acts with integrity. Politically unaware.
Fox	Psychological game player. Politically aware.
Baboon	Psychological game player. Politically unaware.
Dolphin	Acts with integrity. Politically aware.

The behaviour of the four animals is described below.

The SHEEP sees the world through simplistic eyes; he believes you are right if you are in a position of authority. He does what he is told, sticks to the rules, is too busy to network and doesn't know how to build coalitions and alliances. He acts with integrity but is street naïve.

The FOX knows exactly what is going on but uses that knowledge to exploit the weaknesses in others. He is self-centred but with a charming veneer. He is manipulative and likes games involving winners and losers; and loves leading lambs to the slaughterhouse.

The BABOON is not tuned into the grapevine; his antennae are blocked and he therefore ends up conspiring with the powerless. He is emotionally illiterate, seeing things in black and white and not recognising when he is fighting a losing battle. He plays games with people but doesn't understand why he keeps losing.

The DOLPHIN takes account of other people personally, he is an excellent listener and aware of others' viewpoints. He is non-defensive, open and shares information. He uses creativity and imagination to engineer win–win situations. He acts from both an informed and ethical standpoint; he is both streetwise and virtuous.

Inevitably there is a little of all four animal in each of us, dependent upon mood, circumstance and situation. Sometimes the best course of action may be to walk away, which looks like the strategy of the SHEEP; sometimes it does us good to have a whinge and whine with the powerless (i.e., BABOON) or maybe we just need to score that point (i.e., FOX). However, it's all about one's prime strategy.

What characterises the DOLPHIN is calmness in a storm, a certainty about their own destiny and a thirst to learn from others. They may be busy, but not stressed or pressured; and they can always find the time to work alongside senior colleagues on an even footing, trading ideas rather than blows. They have time for people and for learning. People have respect for them as model human beings first, great leaders or role models second and as an IT person third.

Too often the CIO is perceived as a SHEEP, he works hard, keeps his head down, is too busy to network or go beyond his job description and is lacking in the interpersonal skills department. The consequence of such behaviour is the reputation of a "super techie" who becomes a convenient scapegoat when the inevitable happens.

In order to increase their influence, CIOs need to:

- Stop focusing on metrics and benchmarks and start focusing on building relationships and trust.
- Stop analysis paralysis and learn to trust their gut and their heart.
- Stop talking technology and start talking business.
- Stop talking about "educating the users" and start talking about communicating and sharing knowledge with the rest of the business.
- Stop focusing on the nitty-gritty of current issues and start focusing on innovation and the future strategy.
- Stop talking about problems and start talking about possibilities.
- Stop being risk adverse and start making those big strategic decisions where there is no right answer or best practice to follow.
- Stop taking themselves too seriously and start developing their sense of humour.
- Become a leader rather than a follower.

This is DOLPHIN behaviour and the behaviour adopted by 20 CIOs I recently studied who were subsequently promoted to CEO – what could be a better measure of political success?!

Dr Robina Chatham, Visiting Fellow at
Cranfield School of Management

The role of the CIO needs to change. A more strategic focus is required. This has an impact on the lesser known role of Chief Technology Officer.

Sam Lowe, Sector CTO at Capgemini suggests a way forward:

The changing role of the enterprise CTO

Today's enterprise IT departments are increasingly reaching to become more than yesterday's simple service providers. Instead, to moving towards becoming trusted partners for business change. This creates a need for the Head of IT (be it called Chief Information Officer or IT Director) to get closer to, and become more of a partner to the directors of each commercial business unit rather than just a supplier to them. Ultimately in some organisations this means actually becoming part of the executive board itself.

However, this change in level of operation for the CIO can leave a vacuum beneath him or her in many organisations as the previously senior managers of the CIO's IT leadership team need to step up to true director levels of operation. It also changes the demands placed on each member of the IT leadership team in terms of what responsibilities and accountabilities they must have to prosper as a business partner rather than a supplier.

A key example of this is the Chief Technology Officer (CTO); the individual in IT responsible for technology strategy and architecture. Very often these individuals have come from very technical backgrounds such as infrastructure planning or systems design, and have progressed through IT based on their:

- knowledge of the IT industry;
- undoubted intellectual abilities;
- ability to express themselves more clearly than other technical people.

As CIOs become more executive-focussed, they are expected to define what outcomes are required and what the priorities are, committing to key themes. No longer can the CIO himself define and manage the realisation of this, advised by his CTO. He or she now needs the CTO to define and assure its realisation instead.

As a result of this, the needs of the CTO are evolving beyond being a technology-focused advisor decoupled from operations, facing off to the IT vendors. It moves to being a director focused more on business-outcomes, also with accountabilities within IT delivery, and also facing off to internal business-unit leadership teams.

This requires deep technology competency as before, but now with new requirements to communicate and execute effectively with the lines of business, the transformational programmes, and the operational directors within IT. In particular they must articulate themselves in a way that their executive and their customers in the lines of business can understand and value, not just in a way their internal IT colleagues do. The focus is shifting from strategic development to strategic execution – delivering transformation and innovation outcomes, not just creating strategies and roadmaps.

Sam Lowe, Sector CTO, Capgemini

TECHNOLOGY MANAGEMENT

"Any sufficiently advanced technology is indistinguishable from magic."

Sir Arthur C. Clarke, British Author

In this chapter:

- The need for technology management.
- Technology management – why it doesn't happen.
- Towards technology management.
- Technology management – external perspectives.

value management

circulation management

service management

technology management

people entwinement

process entwinement

strategy entwinement

The Need for Technology Management

Technology is where "the rubber hits the road" in respect of IT value optimisation. For many business leaders, technology is a post-school equivalent of their least favourite subject. The very word "technology" can trigger sensations of terror and helplessness. The beauty of being grown up is that one has more control over avoiding such unsavoury matters. Business leaders in general seem to flex their control muscles to avoid anything to do with technology, and in particular their responsibilities in relation to technology.

Technology management is unsurprisingly the most technical of the IT Value Stack layers. So it is not unreasonable that business leaders might shy away from this layer and abdicate it to the IT department. Good governance requires board-level management of all organisational assets. Percentage-wise, technology is a significant enough cost to warrant specific boardroom attention. Having a CIO at board level goes some way to addressing this, but I feel that every board member needs to understand technology sufficiently well to make business-related technology decisions (and technology-related business decisions).

This section makes the case for better technology management as an effective approach to gaining a better return on one's investment in IT.

Keep your distance

As a technologist working for an IT service company, I had the view that customers have no business in attempting to influence technology decisions. My colleagues and I were providing a service. The customer determined what they wanted and we decided how that was to be achieved technically. Customers that interfered in technology matters were seen as a risk to be managed. Our attitude dissuaded users from taking an interest in technology, plus it reinforced the belief that technology was solely the business of technologists. Inadvertently, my generation's enthusiasm for keeping the users at a safe distance played a role in discouraging users from taking an interest in technology. But in our defence, the technologies available then did not lend themselves to dynamic user interaction. Fortunately, the technologies and development techniques have improved, but the users are still hesitant. Hence the very thought of technology management taking place anywhere other than within the IT department is inconceivable to many.

Executives and technology management

But can senior executives side-step technology matters, leaving them as an operational issue for the black-box IT department? Information technology service companies perhaps reveal the answer.

Information technology service companies are no different to end user companies; they are businesses that need to make a profit. The majority of IT service company leaders are not technologists. They do of course need to have a sound understanding of profit, cash flow and risk management; specifically, how all of these relate to technology. Thus they have controls in place to ensure that their technologists focus their attention on what is valuable to the shareholders, without incurring undue risk.

It is my view that business leaders in end user companies need to take the same approach to the management of their own technology assets, given the increasing relationship between IT and business success.

Design advice versus design constraints

Service management exists to protect the users from the nitty-gritty of technology. Most users do not want to concern themselves with technology detail. Do you really need to know how the electricity that fuels your business is produced? So users only need to concern themselves with what and when. "How" is an issue for the service deliverer. Being more service-oriented today, technologists should indulge the users when they make technology-related suggestions and explain in the gentlest of terms that it is best to leave such decisions to the experts. Taking the time to explain why can be considered an investment in IT value optimisation.

But design advice is not the same as design constraints. The users might well articulate what appear to be design imperatives. For example, the database must be browser based and accessible from a palmtop device. Or they may state that the database must be developed using technology X because they have committed to that technology across the organisation and want to minimise the interoperability issues. These are essentially design constraints rather than attempts to interfere in the design, and should be acknowledged and treated with respect. There will need to be a robust technology case if these requirements are going to be overruled.

Users need to have a degree of technology competence to engage with technologists, even at the user–technologist level. Anything less and the technologists will bamboozle the users into submission, if these design constraints prove to be an inconvenience for the IT department. The same happens at board level. The only difference is that the stakes are much higher. Senior executives ultimately need to have the final say on strategic technology matters, even though the recommendation will come from the CIO. The senior executives need a "trust and verify" approach, and that is the essence of technology management.

Technology demystified

There are two main elements to technology management:

- The cost-effective creation/assembly of technologies needed to deliver new services.

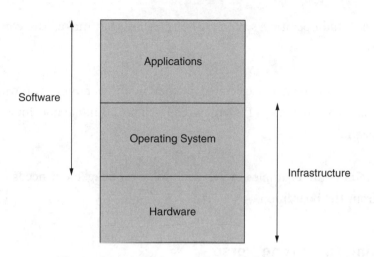

Figure 6.1 Fundamental framework diagram

- The cost-effective maintenance of the technologies needed to deliver the existing services.

For readers who are unfamiliar with what technology really is (see Figure 6.1):

- Technology essentially comprises hardware and software.
- Technology can be classified into front end (user side) and back end (IT department side).
- Technology can also be partitioned into infrastructure (supports the applications) and applications (that deliver the real value to users).

Applications are the stars of the show. They are the tools that enhance user productivity and thus play a direct role in delivering business value. Infrastructure can be considered as those technologies that are needed to enable the applications to run – i.e., hardware (computers, peripherals and networks) and operating systems (the software that makes the computers usable).

That was a somewhat accelerated primer in IT. For more information I encourage you to read "IT Demystified – The IT handbook for business professionals".

What follows are examples of why technology management needs to originate from the boardroom.

Backing the wrong horse

The technology market is in a state of chaos, analogous to the Wild West. Technology management is an exercise in risk management. The vendor of today's hot technology may not exist in a few years' time. No technology vendor is guaranteed a place in the technology end game. The Pac-Man manoeuvres of the major players are redefining the technology landscape on an almost daily basis. Customers do not appear to be the beneficiaries of the vendor battles. You need to understand how to manage the IT department to ensure that your organisation does not back the wrong horse and take the organisation into a technology cul-de-sac. To dampen this risk, many companies back all the horses until an outright winner emerges. This is a lazy and expensive approach. A more informed boardroom might take some calculated risks and make better use of their technology spend.

Business-driven

Technologists love technology. The bigger the organisation the closer the IT department starts to resemble "Toys R Us" in the eyes of the technologists. Well-meaning CIOs have been known to commission systems that they believe to be useful, but a lack of user consultation has led to the equivalent of organ transplant rejection. The CIO then perceives the users as ungrateful and thus becomes less service-oriented in his outlook. Or worse still, they become very service-oriented and stick rigidly to the service-level agreements that have been negotiated to ensure an "adequate at best" service.

Business leaders need to ensure that all technology initiatives are underpinned by a business case. Specifically, there needs to be a boardroom sponsor who will take the associated credit or blame and so will think twice before making a commitment. Once a system is commissioned, the technologists need to take an approach to development that is both user-inclusive and can be delivered on time to meet the associated business window of opportunity. This might be regarded as an operational detail, but it is a major cause of technology misspending. Large-budget, high-impact IT projects should be managed closely from a boardroom perspective because their delay or failure may materially impact the organisation's strategy.

Return on investment

Technologists love new technology. Any opportunity to adopt the latest technologies will be leaped upon. Like everyone else, technologists have one eye on employability and so will seize every opportunity to enhance their résumés. This is something the CIO should be able to keep in check. But the technology vendors, as opposed to the service providers, know that senior executives don't appreciate the nuances of technology offerings and so market to the technologists who then create an upward pressure within the IT department to a point where purchase decisions are made.

Business executives need to ensure that technology purchases are only made when necessary. In fact, the IT department should be encouraged to "make meals out of leftovers". Establish whether the current technology investment can deliver the business requirement. The best CIOs are resourceful and with a little encouragement could save the organisation both time and money. Think asset sweating.

Migrate to simplicity

Very few large organisations have a textbook IT department with a minimalist approach to technology adoption. Mergers and acquisitions have a shredding effect on the CIO's lovingly crafted IT strategy. It is only in recent times that merger and acquisition due diligence has regarded the compatibility of technologies as a variable to consider. Each new technology acquired requires specialist support, which is expensive. Reducing the number of technologies, or even the number of IT departments, down to a suitable number needs to be a priority. Simplicity equates to manageability. It should also improve the return on investment. The CIO's IT strategy document needs to become a "migration to simplicity" plan.

The CIO might actually welcome a detached "helicopter view" on his digital smorgasbord. Being under pressure to maintain service levels, keeping unwelcome visitors out of the network and keeping the boardroom out of prison might prove a distraction from this bigger picture. The boardroom needs to ensure that the IT department reaches the right balance between short- and long-term objectives.

Beyond the technology nuclear winter

Managing technology was easy during the post-dotcom crash. The only IT projects that were commissioned during this "nuclear era" were those that caused the lights to go out in some part of the organisation. Forget innovation; cost reduction was the driver.

The subsequent market upturn has presented the IT department with a myriad of architectural upgrade options, including:

- Choice of application deployment model – for example, web services.
- Choice of application development model – for example, SOA.
- Choice of infrastructure model – for example, grid, utility.

These are tantalising choices for the IT department. All represent a "drains up" architectural overhaul.

The key question is whether these approaches represent fads or the future. And if they represent the future, how soon into the future will they move from fiction to fact?

I would not expect senior business executives to be subject matter experts in respect of architectures. However, I would expect them to ensure that the IT department is making architectural decisions based on hard evidence rather than marketing hype.

Rationale Summary

Technology management on first inspection may not seem an appropriate matter for the boardroom. But some technology decisions have such profound implications on the business that abdicating responsibility to the IT department constitutes gross mismanagement. Today the boardroom may find technology a distasteful distraction from core business. But as competitive advantage, cost management, service delivery, good governance and risk management are increasingly achieved using IT, then senior executives who are not comfortable with technology management will be of limited value to their shareholders.

Technology Management – Why it Doesn't Happen

At best, technology management happens within the IT department. As suggested in the previous section, this needs to be managed from the top of the organisation – particularly where technology spend is a significant percentage of revenue, or is critical to the customer experience. As mentioned, most boardrooms treat IT and the IT department as a "black box" and so most business executives are happy to let the technologists worry about the "how"; at best they just concern themselves with the service element of the IT department's output.

This section identifies some of the issues that have led to the boardroom opting out of this critical element of IT value management.

Information technology is not that important

Senior executives have a daunting array of responsibilities, which are all in some way related to delivering shareholder value. Traditionally, IT was not seen as critical to shareholder value. And there is still a relatively influential school of thought that believes IT has no role to play in this respect. It is indeed true that there is no competitive advantage in using Microsoft Word, though there is the potential of competitive disadvantage in not using Microsoft Word if your business involves electronic document transfer with clients who do.

Email and other hygiene applications also fall into this category. As a result the IT department has struggled to get the attention of the board, being seen as an infrastructural necessity, much like the phone and the central heating. However, there is a link between corporate governance and IT governance. Poor controls as a result of poor IT systems constitute poor governance. Poor governance has severe consequences for the boardroom. Conversely, good governance will enhance shareholder value, as clients and investors migrate to the best-governed organisations. Thus IT does have a role to play in enhancing shareholder value. Not all business leaders have made this connection, and are thus happy to leave IT to someone else down the food chain.

Amongst those who believe that IT is of boardroom significance there is a subset who believe that IT can be managed by just one of the executive team. Where there isn't a CIO on board the responsibility will be delegated to the CFO or COO. This approach unburdens the other board members from having to consider IT issues. Given that IT permeates all business functions, and has a significant role to play in the performance of those functions, it is a problem that some board members feel IT in general, and technology management in particular, is not their concern.

Information technology doesn't make sense

It is understandable that senior executives avoid IT matters, though it is not acceptable. Technologists seem to speak a foreign language that appears to have little to do with business. Many senior executives have carved a career path to the top that has had little or no overlap with the IT department. Consequently, they have not developed an appreciation of how IT works and the associated issues and responsibilities. Having majored in sales or finance, they would much rather opine on matters where they feel they can add genuine value, and thus have no wish to become embroiled in technology matters. An IT-ignorant board is unlikely to provide wise technology leadership. This is a problem for shareholders.

Boardroom ill-equipped to manage IT

As mentioned, many senior executives are ill-equipped to influence techno-logy matters within their organisation. This leads to unpredictable consequences in respect of:

* **Security** – the role of IT in security is increasing dramatically. Poor technology management at board level will lead to inaccurate threat assessments.

- **Governance** – the quality of the systems that contribute to good governance will vary unless good system engineering practices are in place and being monitored at the highest levels. The approach taken by the IT industry in general in respect of software "engineering" leaves a lot to be desired, and thus poses a major risk to IT-centric organisations.
- **Performance** – the expectations of the boardroom and those of the IT department are unlikely to coincide if the strategic requirements in respect of technology performance are not clearly understood by all parties.

Traditional approaches to system development have resulted in system development lifecycles operating on a different clock cycle to the needs of the business. Consequently, systems are delivered late and in many cases are no longer relevant to the business needs, which have evolved since the system was first specified. This is tremendously wasteful and demoralising for both users and technologists; tension mounts and the associated IT value plummets into negative figures.

Poor traceability between the business strategy and what actually happens within the IT department is also a source of problems. This happens when the IT department is left to its own devices.

The IT department knows best

We all dream of a time when we are not under the scrutiny of a manager, and so generally do not encourage our managers to tighten the reins if they have become too slack. The lack of boardroom intervention in respect of technology matters suits the IT department for this reason, and also because clueless managers are actually a danger to "progress". So, almost by mutual consent the boardroom has left the IT department alone. A lack of direction coupled with a desire to be useful results in IT departments developing systems that they believe will be of value to the business, but without going through a formal approval/business case process.

Data warehouses are a good example of a potentially useful (and expensive) technology that the IT department has built to capture the data it feels the business needs. Unfortunately, through a lack of consultation this is unlikely to be what the business actually needs. Much like having a Christmas present derided, the IT department becomes hurt and loses interest in being helpful. Once the technologists become disillusioned it is unlikely that the organisation will get good value from its IT investment.

Information technology vendors too influential

As mentioned earlier, the technology vendors exert their influence via the technologists. But certain technology vendors have recognised that in general business executives do not have a great interest in technology. These smart technology vendors have redefined their offerings in terms of business-relevant services. It strikes me as odd that a technology hardware vendor can present itself as an expert in HR outsourcing, but I appreciate that it is an easier sell to the board than hawking a batch of servers.

Having got into the boardroom, the vendors will launch a charm offensive, which might include an expenses-free trip to their research and development laboratories to witness the latest business "disruptive" "killer apps". Having been wined and dined (and brainwashed), the replete executives return to the business and summon the CIO to inform him of the future of new technologies and that he must change direction immediately in order to capitalise on the technologies offered by vendor X. The CIO nods obediently, but his heart is sinking. It is hard to swallow that this external vendor has got more influence over technology strategy than he has.

Naïve executives are a technology risk.

Poor understanding of the technologist's mindset

Business executives are usually smart, commercial and politically aware. Technologists are often intellectually smart, but less often emotionally smart. They are also not always commercial and rarely political. Business executives who attempt to manage technologists, including CIOs, as if they were a lesser or evolving version of themselves will be unsuccessful.

Technologists are different, for example:

- Technologists love technology and sometimes see it as an end in itself rather than an enabler of business productivity. Some technologists actually race home from work and then spend all evening and perhaps all night working on software for free. This makes no sense to business people.
- Technologists like problems and challenges. Playing down what is required of them will actually dampen their enthusiasm rather than curb their anxieties. Technologists have a tendency to over-engineer where they can. Why build a scooter when you can build a Porsche? Vague business requirements will lead to over-engineered solutions that will invariably be more expensive, delivered late and more prone to errors.
- Technologists like to be in control, and often perceive users as a threat in this respect. Business people will find they have greater influence over technologists if they can make the technologists feel as though they are in the driving seat. Irritating, I know, but who said managing techies was easy?

- Technologists generally make poor people managers. Technologist-led teams are often dysfunctional, as the leader is more focused on dominance than optimised solutions using the expertise of all team members.

Until technologists become more rounded individuals, business leaders need to factor the above in when dealing with the IT department. All of these apparent weaknesses, if well managed, could be turned into value-enhancing activity. A lack of attention in this respect will prove equally value-dampening.

Problem Summary

A lack of boardroom IT representation is the surest way to minimise the value obtained from your IT investment. Isolating technology management to one member of the board is likely to lead to the underperformance of one's IT assets, given that IT is strategically important to all board members. The traditional career path of many board members has made them technology-averse. This is a fundamental problem that, if not addressed, will negatively impact all stakeholders.

Towards Technology Management

Boardroom-driven technology management is key to yielding business value from the IT investment. It signals:

- To shareholders that you are managing company assets effectively.
- To customers that you are both innovative and focused on value.
- To regulators that you take compliance seriously.

Technology management is not something that many business leaders feel comfortable with. But the world is changing and this presents an opportunity for those business leaders prepared to take on this new responsibility. Good technology management does not require technical skill, but it does require the ability to focus on what is important.

This section provides guidance on how to enhance the return on your IT investment by proactive technology management.

Invest in boardroom development

This point was made in the previous section. But given that the need is particularly acute in respect of technology management, it is mentioned again. The IT department may feel a little threatened by the new-found interest of the boardroom. Over time, technology-aware business leaders will inspire confidence in the technologists, who are then more likely to see the value in receiving "external" guidance.

Invest in IT management

Technology management essentially boils down to generating the maximum return on the technology assets; these assets include both technologists and technology. Developing the technologists to both manage other technologists and managing technology is required. HR needs to put processes in place to identify technologists with the potential to be good people managers and then to provide them with the appropriate skills.

Good technology and people management potential are difficult to find in the one body. So consider making certain critical positions such as chief technology officer a multi-person role. One person can be the technology expert (big brain in a conical flask), the other can be the people manager.

Engage with technologists

Good managers interact with their people. Great managers care for their people. Identify your most valuable technologists and get to know them. Praise them publicly and reward them. I am not suggesting that you sidestep or undermine the CIO, but that you and your colleagues make the effort to treat your best IT performers as you would your best sales people. Whilst it may seem unlikely today, as the world becomes more IT-centric, one of these tech stars may well be a future CEO in waiting. And do not forget to involve the IT department when considering takeover targets.

Pin down migration strategy

Many large organisations got that way through acquisitions. Each acquisition brought a fresh, and sometimes a not-so-fresh, array of technologies to support. Each technology requires specialist support staff. These people can work out expensive if the associated technologies offer only marginal value to the business.

Reducing the number of technologies and thus the associated skills (i.e., people) required is a priority. The IT department's strategy must clearly indicate how the migration process will take place. Their challenge is to define what the technology profile will look like when this is complete, whilst knowing that new business-changing technologies will emerge that will impact this profile. Let the technologists worry about this. You simply need to monitor whether the overall trend is towards a narrowing of your technology investment spectrum.

Implement system development best practice

If your organisation needs to develop its own software then best practice must be in place. Software development is a complex art/science. Many IT departments regard software development, in particular programming, as something new starters do, and thus ambitious technologists are keen to move onto loftier pursuits. Thus programming is in the main carried out by inexperienced people. This is a recipe for software problems that can often result in serious business problems.

One approach is to make software development a worthy career path by rewarding accordingly. The second approach is to put best practice in place to dumb down the process sufficiently so that software development can be carried out by less experienced staff. Keep in mind that software reuse is important, so this is to be encouraged. As is keeping the users involved in the development process; the lack of which has led to many high profile and expensive failures. Read up on object orientation and agile methods for more details.

In broad terms I would discourage software development, whether that be in-house or outsourced. Bespoke software development is expensive. You incur all the development costs. It takes for ever, and when you eventually receive the software it doesn't work because you are the first to really test it. Scour the market for existing products that will meet your needs, or for configurable solutions that meet most of your needs. With the latter in mind it is sometimes cheaper to mould your business processes to the most reliable ready-to-use solutions.

Implement IT operations best practice

The bulk of the IT budget is spent on keeping the existing systems available to users. In a market downturn typically zero budget is allocated to development. The world of IT operations (aka support) is relatively mature. Best practice is available "off the shelf" in both proprietary and non-proprietary forms. You are encouraged to encourage your IT department to avoid reinventing the wheel and adopt (and, if necessary, tune) a tried and tested approach.

The IT department should run like an efficient hotel. Every aspect of support needs to be procedurised. This will both reduce the associated risks and reduce the IT department payroll bill. If necessary, spend money on hiring in expertise to put these procedures in place. Also, ensure that your IT department's disaster recovery procedures are also in place. And remember not to have your disaster recovery team based in the one building.

Set up a research laboratory

New technologies are not that far removed from the science that inspired them. Some new technologies are so new and untested that it would be wise to ensure your organisation is fully clear on their strengths and weaknesses before they are woven into the organisational fabric. Similarly, it is wise to check the interoperability of technologies in isolation before committing to their integration with your existing technology investment. Certain emerging technologies must be monitored so that your organisation can adopt them quickly if the market or business conditions necessitate it. Thus, it is prudent to allocate some of your IT budget to technology exploration.

Avoid proprietary standards

This is not always practical, but it is something to strive for. Proprietary standards are standards that are under the control of a single vendor. Adopt these standards and your fortunes are now entwined with those of the technology vendor. Press the IT department to adopt open standards (not to be confused with open source, though there is some overlap – the former are standards that are usually controlled by an international standards body, the latter is a counterintuitive approach to developing software. Depending on who you speak to, open source will be regarded as either good or bad. In my view the notion is noble, the practice is variable and to use it is to become a pawn in the war between two of the world's major IT players.)

Very new technologies are rarely based on open standards. The older the new technology, the more likely it will conform to vendor-independent standards. This is a major reason for avoiding new technologies. Ensure that you do not commit your organisation to being an unpaid vendor test site.

Keep vendors at bay

Some thoughts:

- Technology vendors need to be managed. Ensure that the CIO and the chief technologists are involved in vendor selection.
- Ensure your organisation has representation on the user groups associated with your major suppliers.
- Avoid adopting bleeding-edge technologies, unless you are conscious of the associated risks. Being an early adopter of a new, soon to be defunct, technology (not all new IT solutions will have a long and healthy life-cycle) will be costly in attracting the appropriate support staff and may leave you in a technology cul-de-sac.
- Once you have established that your major vendors are trustworthy, treat them as partners. There comes a point where you both need each other. Good partners will be more flexible, so hopefully the relationship will extend beyond rigid service level agreements.

Consider outsourcing

Outsourcing, and particularly offshoring, is a consequence of globalisation. It makes economic sense to outsource aspects of your business if the vendor can deliver more cheaply to a similar, if not higher, standard. "Big-bang hand it all over" outsourcing is reckless. A portfolio of suppliers has its downsides but ultimately spreads your risk. Offshoring is not delivering the cost savings that many organisations hoped for, but it has the potential to deliver some savings.

The question to consider is whether IT is so important to your business that it should be handed over to professionals or whether it is so important to your business that you must retain total control of it (through your own in-house IT professionals). If you pursue the outsourcing/offshoring path, ensure that you outsource your activities and not your controls.

Be sensitive to your IT department. Don't charge into outsourcing because your peers in similar organisations are doing it. I suggest you give your IT department first refusal on the work to be outsourced. The CIO may welcome this move. If not, then she should be given the option to submit an alternative bid for boardroom consideration. Keep total cost of ownership (TCO) in mind when assessing whether to outsource your IT assets to a third party.

Sweat the technology

Before the IT department steers you into buying more technology, ensure that all other options have been explored. Technology performance optimisation is a growth market. There are plenty of vendors that will help you get more from your applications and infrastructure.

Action Summary

Good management is key to getting the best from your technology investment. As we have seen, business leaders have a valuable role to play in technology management, despite not being technologists. Smart CIOs will recognise that having access to board-level resources will make their role easier, and it will help keep IT on the boardroom agenda.

Technology Management – External Perspectives

This section provides an alternative view to my own in respect of technology management. The contributors were asked to answer one or more of the following questions:

- Why is technology management important?
- Why is this not generally being addressed?
- What are the underlying problems?
- What are the consequences of failing to address this issue?
- What advice would you give in respect of technology management?

Why is technology management important?

At Alliance Boots we are focused on providing good value for the customer. This requires continuous reduction of our cost base, and that includes the cost base of our IT department.

Poor technology management, whether it be underpinning confidential patient information or product manufacture, will lead to a diminished customer experience and reputational damage. Thus technology management is critical.

Rob Fraser, IT Director, Alliance Boots

Providing for the technology needs of the business is after all the reason that the IT department exists, so supporting the business is core. In essence this means providing the business solutions, information and service levels that the business needs, in a predictable, managed professional manner.

But beyond this it also means planning a technology and architecture portfolio that is flexible enough so as not to be a constraint to new business demands or initiatives, whilst not unduly impacting IT's ability to deliver reliably. In parallel the IT department must continually endeavour to reduce the cost and resource requirements of "keeping the lights on".

But even beyond this, IT departments also have to deal with technology baggage that adds no value to the business, such as:

- Managing increasingly complex technology infrastructures and license agreements.
- Keeping up to date with increasingly short technology lifecycles.
- Keeping on top of relationships with an increasingly competitive and dynamic technology vendor marketplace.

Sam Lowe, Sector CTO, Capgemini

It is important to have the right balance for the company and its culture. Do you need to replace your PCs every year? Of course not. But to some companies this is so very important. Not so much from an IT point of view but from an image point of view. Woe betide the IT director who gets it wrong!

Vivian Ash, Group Information Manager, BASF

IT makes modern businesses tick. Without it most businesses would not survive. To comply with the increasingly onerous demands of corporate governance requires good technology management. In particular this means that the underlying IT architectures and management information systems must be clear, joined-up, efficient and provide the data needed to demonstrate compliance. IT governance is crucial. Most organisations need to ensure they have strong management of their software, hardware and data.

Steve Tyler, UK Programmes Director, LogicaCMG

Technology management is like any other business area. It can be efficient or inefficient with consequential cost implications. It also has business risk implications. It can bankrupt a business if there is not enough and stifle innovation if there is too much.

Nick Leake, Director of Operations and Infrastructure, ITV

Why is this not generally being addressed?

There are of course many reasons. A lack of business management can lead to poor technology management. We have found that business drivers such as the need to reduce our cost base in support of the business strategy have helped keep our focus in this respect. Also, regulatory compliance has encouraged us to ensure that our house is in order.

Rob Fraser, IT Director, Alliance Boots

It is difficult to achieve the correct balance between the processes associated with providing the operational IT service and delivering new IT projects, with those associated with the strategic processes of managing the IT architectures and managing the portfolio of IT programmes.

Different stakeholders are involved on each side and have different skills-sets, viewpoints and motivations. And yet, all the processes intertwine when it comes to technology management as they all act on, or utilise, the same technology that serves the same business at different phases of its lifecycle.

If the balance is wrong, or if the necessary governing frameworks are incomplete, then it will always be extremely difficult to turn destructive conflict between different motivations into the creative conflict needed to improve the state of the technology and its ability to respond to what's demanded of it.

Many organisations unfortunately have not sufficiently reassessed their technology management frameworks and processes, and are still persisting with ones from their past or the pasts of their employees. New technology demands and approaches (e.g., the much discussed service-oriented architecture or SOA) require concerted management from all sides. The risk is that these organisations will now find themselves trying to navigate without much of the necessary information, capability and control.

Sam Lowe, Sector CTO, Capgemini

IT assets are often fragmented throughout an organisation and are changing all the time.

Steve Tyler, UK Programmes Director, LogicaCMG

Technology moves so quickly it is hard to optimise it once it is deployed. Once stabilised, the sub-optimal failings come to light and the next upgrade is required.

Nick Leake, Director of Operations and Infrastructure, ITV

What are the underlying problems?

I can imagine that a disconnect between the business and the IT department, such that there is no clear correlation between their activities, could well lead to a casual approach to technology management.

Rob Fraser, IT Director, Alliance Boots

Most large organisations have completed several generations of system/technology deployment and consolidation. This has mostly led to a trend towards bigger and more capable systems and platforms to make better use of advances in technology for specific business areas. It has also led to projects growing in scale and to more industrialised project approaches, which are largely focused on operational efficiencies.

However, bigger and more efficient systems, platforms and projects can only go so far. Many portfolios still have service costs that are too high, which leads to a lack of resources directed towards improving the portfolio. In particular, the level of effort and relative cost of change is now very high as most organisations are reliant on unsustainable legacy systems for certain parts of their estate. Increasingly we are witnessing duplicated, complex and interdependent clusters of systems built around more modern technologies.

IT departments have in the past had difficulties at planning technology at the enterprise level (rather than at the project level) in terms of the business value it provides. Too often the indirect business cases and technology-centric culture of IT departments have meant that technology characteristics have been the decision-making criteria at the enterprise level, with the people who know the most about the technology steering the decision making. This has often meant that the enterprise-level technology strategy lacks credibility given the poor collaboration between the IT department and business. On occasion the technology strategy has had its relevance openly challenged, when IT implementation projects have chosen alternative technologies in order to meet the needs of the business.

Sam Lowe, Sector CTO, Capgemini

Technology needs to become more mature and stable. Upgrades need to happen less frequently.

Nick Leake, Director of Operations and Infrastructure, ITV

What are the consequences of failing to address this issue?

This lack of an integrated and business-driven view across areas such as strategy, architecture, delivery and support makes it difficult to reconcile the enterprise view of technology with that of individual IT projects.

This in turn constrains the IT department's ability to coordinate its technologies within and across different parts of its business. It also constrains IT's ability to converse and hence collaborate with the business as a partner for change. Ultimately it constrains the business's ability to respond to industry pressures or to use technology to innovate, which is now a necessity for many industries in today's marketplace.

Sam Lowe, Sector CTO, Capgemini

Anything from minor weaknesses to disaster and bankruptcy.

Nick Leake, Director of Operations and Infrastructure, ITV

What advice would you give in respect of addressing this issue?

Adopt good/best practice within the IT department. Listen to the advice of your audit function. Ensure there is activity traceability and controls in place.

We have learned a lot from our experiences of outsourcing, and ultimately this is proving to be a successful approach. Key lessons include:

- The outsourcer's framework must reflect that of the business. So not only must there be alignment of IT with the business, there needs to be alignment between the IT department's strategic suppliers and the business.
- Use a utility outsourcing model as this continuously encourages the IT department to improve the performance of its applications so as to use less data storage and processing power. Thus reducing the utility bill. This has the impact of reducing the overall cost of IT. In fact in our case this discipline has led to a 40 % reduction in our server base in the last three years.

Rob Fraser, IT Director, Alliance Boots

Firstly, many organisations need to consider how they can improve their focus in respect of the business-value technology can deliver. And then to use this business-value focus to improve the IT department's engagement with the business.

Beyond that, organisations can then consider how they adopt architectural standardisation within their IT in addition to the technology standardisation they've been working (or in some cases struggling) with to date. This is necessary to move beyond consolidating and exploiting systems and platforms to creating a workable managed enterprise framework of services, components and information that are focused on what is being provided rather than just the implementation.

Within IT project delivery, the quality, visibility of cost and management of complexity can be improved through ongoing access to information about the enterprise's IT assets and their dependencies. Furthermore, the incorporation of asset and design-level governance procedures into the historically operationally focused project delivery management methodologies gives a far better balance between the enterprise-view of "big-picture" and the project-view of expedited delivery. Fundamentally though, in order to reduce the cost and time required for businesses to innovate or respond with IT, the average project size, cost and duration needs to come down. This can be achieved through working with a larger number of smaller projects, which in turn generally requires a common portfolio view of programme investments to enable federated coordination and management.

Overall it is likely that IT departments need to re-evaluate their required capabilities and skill-sets moving forward to address some of these challenges. But they also need to fundamentally reconsider the operational and strategic processes they are using, and the methods of management, governance and incentivisation involved. Just changing the resource mix and imposing compliance-based governance procedures is unlikely to be enough without more fundamental changes in behaviours.

Sam Lowe, Sector CTO, Capgemini

You have to allocate sufficient resources to technology management whilst at the same time recognising that it can never be perfect.

Nick Leake, Director of Operations and Infrastructure, ITV

SERVICE MANAGEMENT

"The man who gives little with a smile gives more than the man who gives much with a frown."

Jewish Proverb

In this chapter:

- The need for service management.
- Service management – why it doesn't happen.
- Towards service management.
- Service management – external perspectives.

value management

circulation management

service management

technology management

people entwinement

process entwinement

strategy entwinement

The Need for Service Management

Whilst this book is promoting the notion that the IT department is an equal to the business, there is no escaping the fact that on a day-to-day basis it is providing a service, and so must behave accordingly. The quality of that service will determine the users' perception of the IT department, much in the same way as a restaurant's service will determine the diner's perception of the kitchen. A good kitchen fronted by surly waiters undermines the chef's endeavours. Increasingly, the IT department is providing a service to both users and customers. A lack of service will impinge on client loyalty and thus revenues.

This section explores the notion that better IT service leads to an improved return on the IT investment.

IT needs to get business-like

The IT department is faced with competition from outsourcers across the globe. Your IT department needs to understand that and respond to the threat by constantly demonstrating that it is the most valuable supplier of new technology services to the business. The IT department needs to think of itself as a restaurant with the users as diners. The focus needs to be on the experience users have when they use the service.

The service the IT department delivers will be constrained by the budget available or the amount their customers are willing to pay. It is worth keeping in mind that nobody likes poor restaurants, including the staff. Some people like expensive restaurants, but usually as an occasional experience, and often to make a statement about their refined tastes. Most people take greatest pride in using, and perhaps most importantly recommending, restaurants that offer great value. For your IT department to become that great value restaurant you will need your IT people to become more business-like. This goes beyond learning to be nice to users, and on to identifying who the best customers are and lavishing them with the limited love and attention available. This is also known as resource optimisation.

Good service is also defined by the consistency of the experience. Thus the IT department needs to put processes in place to ensure this. As well as consistency, a service ethic will force technologists to think about:

* Quality of service
  - Am I delivering to a consistently high standard?
  - What is that standard, and how is it measured?
* Performance
  - How quickly am I expected to respond to user requests?
* Reliability
  - What is an acceptable failure rate?
* Availability
  - Are users expecting 24 × 7 access?
* Security
  - To what extent do the applications and user data need to be secured?
* Usability
  - What are the users' expectations in terms of engaging with the IT department?
  - Do they expect an advisory or just-fix service?
  - Do they expect the helpdesk to respond within a certain number of phone rings?

Most CIOs recognise the benefits of having a service ethic, though not all have converted the above considerations into a set of unambiguous key performance indicators through which the performance of the IT department can be measured.

Users want service not technology

When I hear the car mechanic talking about the innards of the engine, I move from comfortable to vulnerable. I now have no idea what she is talking about, and therefore I cannot probe the assertions in order to avoid being ripped off. Technologists do not necessarily have that unethical aim in mind, but that doesn't stop the users feeling the same way when the technologist launches into techno-babble. How the IT department delivers the service or resolves my problem is their concern. Users typically don't want to hear the detail. An exception to this is when showing gratitude to a technologist, where for example they have fixed your PDA. Ask them how they managed to fix it. They will launch into detail that you will not necessarily understand, but you are giving them an opportunity to demonstrate their prowess, and that is reward enough for many technologists.

Users do not trust technologists who appear to hide behind buzzwords, and that demeans the perceived value of the service.

Resources need to be used intelligently

Businesses typically invest a relatively high proportion of turnover in IT assets. Good value is achieved when those assets are sweated to the maximum, and focused on supporting the business imperatives. The challenge is compounded by the fact that the technology assets are fast depreciating and are not used optimally. (As you read this book, sleep, take lunch, meet colleagues and so on, the only value your desktop computer offers is providing the capability of an inefficient room heater.)

Similarly, your organic assets – i.e., technologists – need to be constantly reskilled to keep up with the rate of change of technology, never mind having to keep pace with the rate of change of your business. The restaurant maxim, "a soda customer today could be a diner tomorrow" does not apply. The IT department has only so much love to give, and so it needs to be allocated intelligently to where it will make the most positive impact on the business.

A service ethic will enable the IT department to understand what and who is most critical to the business and so channel its resources accordingly.

Easier to deliver real value

Elaborating on the last point, the business will see the IT department as valuable if their engagement is having a material impact on the business. A service mindset will encourage the IT department to engage proactively with the users. If the IT department is simply a reactive service then it is not surprising that users will perceive the IT department in a negative light, only becoming important when there is a problem. If you think this is stretching the association, think about the last time you called the IT helpdesk just to thank them for getting you out of a bind. That's right, there was no last time. It doesn't matter that a technologist has performed a heroic act for you, it is likely that you will perceive technologists in much the same light as plumbers and electricians in respect of your domestic infrastructural challenges. The fact that your problem highlighted your ignorance does not help. For example, when you are advised that your PC will work more effectively if you actually turn on your monitor; irritating, but helpful nonetheless.

A service provider that not only keeps in touch to ensure that all is okay, but sits down and engages with you in respect of your forthcoming plans, is one that will be highly valued. Reactive is not enough.

It gives the CIO career options

As business becomes more IT-centric, it is more likely that the CIO will sit on the board, and eventually more likely that the CIO will become the CEO. So thinking ahead, anything that encourages the CIO to think in business terms is a good thing. A service ethic turns the IT department into a service business, with real costs, assets and customers. What better environment to develop the skills needed for business leadership?

Turn costs into profit

Not everyone believes that IT spend should be considered as an investment. The IT industry's track record to date does not totally support this perspective. But what if the IT department was transformed from money vortex to cash generator? Turning the IT department into a standalone and reliable service unit will benefit both your organisation and perhaps those who are in the same business as you, but further down the rankings. In other words, your IT department could open its doors to other businesses that do not have your economies of scale. All of a sudden the IT department becomes a profit centre, providing white-label IT services to external clients. Your IT department can now use its surplus funds to research innovative ways of keeping your business at the top of the league.

A service mindset makes this possible. And all of a sudden the technologists move from being ancillary overheads to star performers. You have all the benefits associated with outsourcing, whilst retaining genuine expertise in your business, plus they are genuinely under your control. So why not turn your IT department into a business?

Technologists need to know who the customer is

In my first IT role, initially I did not know who the customer was, nor did I even know for what purpose the system was being built. This might have been a reflection of my indifference or inability to see the big picture, but I would like to think it was because I was working on a 500-person project, and nobody felt it necessary that I should have the big picture. And back in those days, higher management might have seen exposing the customer to this vast pool of techies as something of a risk.

Not all projects are of that size, but I meet a lot of technologists who still don't know or care who their customer is. They believe the customer is someone who deals with the sales department, not realising that the IT department has customers too, namely the users. Having a clear understanding of whom we serve, and what excites them in respect of our capabilities, is critical to delivering real value. User indifference is a value-dampener. A service ethic will flush out this attitude dysfunction.

Better service promotes better people entwinement

If users sense that the IT department is contributing to their productivity then they are more likely to treat technologists with respect. In turn, technologists are likely to raise their game. Synergistic relationships between users and technologists underpin leveraging good value from one's IT investment. The ball is in the IT department's court. A service-focused approach is a big step towards maximising business value from your staff on both sides of the IT–business fence.

Better service promotes better process entwinement

As suggested earlier in the book, the IT department has much more to offer than just technology skills. Through building IT systems, technologists find themselves becoming expert in business processes. Some IT departments do not realise that this is something of value to the business. A service-based approach will both reveal this to the IT department and encourage it to package and deliver their process wisdom accordingly.

Rationale Summary

There are clearly many good reasons for the IT department adopting a service-oriented approach. The challenge is in putting a service management framework in place to deliver consistency. Adopting best practice methodologies in respect of IT department processes is a big step in the right direction. However, unless the technologists and their leaders buy into the service ethic, all good/best practice endeavours will generate more heat than action.

Service Management – Why it Doesn't Happen

We have established that an improved service ethic from the IT department will lead to better business value from the IT investment. This is not breakthrough thinking, so why is it that so many users feel the service they receive from the IT department is in the main substandard?

A clearer understanding of service

First let us scope the challenge. We all know that the world's most luxurious hotels have understood the concept of service. They take customer-centricity to new heights, using information they capture relating to our "special needs", and use it (and IT) to heighten the experience – perhaps even extrapolating their captured information to move beyond the reactive to the advisory. We all have a lot to learn from the luxury leisure industry.

Many IT departments are unaware that this is a model to which they should aspire. In the minds of many IT staff they relate more to the emergency services, in that a good day is one in which there were no abusive phone calls or physical assaults on the IT staff. So it is no wonder that the luxury hotel analogy sounds like some sort of fantasy held only by those who do not work on the front line. True. Nobody actually needs a luxury service. However, the idea of the first hotel employee you speak to in respect of a problem becoming the owner and the point of contact for that problem is compelling. So there is relevance in the analogy.

But the hotel analogy in fact doesn't go far enough in my opinion. It is not enough to make the users feel they are being served well. Many users do not necessarily know what is good for them, when their needs are looked at from a global battlefield perspective. Being a little old-fashioned, a military user might well insist that a crossbow is what they require, until they enter the battlefield. Once the user realises that there has been rapid progress in military hardware and the "competition" has kept up with this trend, there will be a brief period of regret prior to his demise. If only he had listened to the technologists back at the "office". If only they hadn't signed up to the "customer is always right" maxim.

My point is that until the users become more expert in IT, the IT market and the impact of IT on their organisation, the IT department's service needs to be a mixture of luxury hotel and army boot camp. This is a tricky if not impossible situation for the IT department to find itself in. It is unlikely that the IT department can truly raise its game in the eyes of the users, until the users have raised their game. Users have a large part to play in the poor service they receive from the IT department.

IT department not run by a business person

Many IT departments are run by technology-centric individuals. They have arrived at the position of CIO via hands-on and project management roles. Their credibility with their staff is typically very good; technologists tend to respect people that truly understand the issues they face.

A background in project management should prepare one for being business-centric. Project management is a broad church, but at the sharp end its adherents develop sound accounting, commercial, leadership and administrative skills. The fixed-price nature of most IT projects today, coupled with the complexity of technology, leads to the project manager being less customer-centric than they would perhaps like to be. And the concept of marketing rarely arises in the context of project management.

In my experience, a background in project management does pave the way to being a competent CIO. But the nature of projects causes project managers and ex-project managers to see the world as a collection of projects/ tasks that have to be achieved/ticked off in a certain time frame within a certain budget. That type of thinking does not always sit well with board members. Market share, governance, profit and loss can be considered as projects of a sort, but the nature of business leadership is less compartmentalised as executive agenda items tend to overlap. Thus, boardroom dialogues tend to appear more chaotic to the project-oriented CIO. Conversely, business leaders can find project-focused thinking as inflexible and inappropriate when discussing strategic matters.

Thus, some CIOs are considered to be lacking in business focus, unable to get their heads around the fact that all roads lead to one business imperative, which is typically a variant of increased shareholder value. Despite a track record of project success, executive colleagues can perceive the CIO as not business-oriented. All business people, from small start-ups through to global leaders, think in terms of profit, sales, marketing and the customer experience. Whilst CIOs actively play a part in all of these areas, they do not necessarily consider these as critical reference points in respect of their own roles.

The head of catering services and the head of real-estate services both have similar roles to play in the success of the business. The former could enhance the return on staff productivity through a health-based nutrition strategy, but state of the art in that field appears to be "food-induced illness" avoidance. The latter can and often does have a major role to play in balance sheet/cash flow health. It could be argued that for many businesses, particularly in retail, the head of real-estate services is more important to business growth than the head of IT, though technology is playing a part in reducing this influence through hot-desking and remote working.

In any case, many CIOs view the world in a different manner to that of their executive colleagues/bosses, and this ultimately leads to a disparity between what the business needs from IT as a service and what it gets.

IT department doesn't have a service ethic

IT departments are at varying stages of maturity in respect of being service-oriented. Some technologists see the user as the enemy, or at least as someone who is disdainful of the IT department. Poor system development techniques coupled with poor pricing models, coupled with poorly educated users leads to conflict between the users and the IT department. Under these siege conditions it is difficult to adopt a service ethic. The above issues are all being addressed to varying degrees, but many technologists are hardened by their formative experiences and it will take some time before their (jaundiced) influence is flushed out of the IT department.

The reputation the IT industry has "built" for itself tars all technologists with the same brush, regardless of their service orientation. Again, this negativity makes it very difficult for technologists to adopt a customer-centric attitude. To change the perceptions of the users requires nothing less than an "all out" charm offensive. Reliable delivery would do no harm either. This does not look set to happen any time soon, not least because the charm gene does not appear consistently in technologist DNA.

Ill-defined requirements

Unsophisticated users of IT are unlikely to have service levels in place with respect to their IT needs. Unfortunately, there are many unsophisticated users within many "sophisticated" organisations. Their inability to articulate their requirements, or their naïveté in terms of what the IT department can deliver, leads to a major breakdown in the IT value flow. The IT department does have a responsibility to help these users become more sophisticated, but the trust levels are generally not high enough for the IT department to lead this initiative.

Indian outsourcers have learnt this to their cost. Winning business in the West has highlighted to them the problems associated with users that think they know what they want, and even with those that do know what they want but don't know how to articulate this need to the supplier. Consequently, Western business users become upset when they discover that they got what they asked for rather than what they needed.

The problem arises from a heady combination of the fixed-price paradigm, where the requirements constitute a contract, and the fact that users generally do not know how to articulate their needs such that IT people will interpret them in an unambiguous manner. Much like a retailer asking for a consignment of T-shirts where the arms are specified as 10 m long instead of 10 cm. The supplier assumes that buyers know what they want and is always right, so goes ahead and produces to this specification. Both buyers and sellers of offshoring services are learning this the hard way.

Service levels are not in the interests of the IT department

Some IT departments are in no hurry to be cornered into performing to a certain level. Whilst IT is not quite science, it is not far off. So demanding a scientist to make three profitable discoveries per year looks fine on paper, but does not reflect the uncertainty that accompanies scientific research. Many IT departments secretly do not buy into the delivery dates that the business has committed them to, and so IT projects overrun.

Service level agreements promote adequacy and not innovation

If IT is to be considered solely as a tool for driving out costs then it is easy to specify to the IT department or outsourcer that their service must do one or more of the following:

- Deliver the same service year on year at ever-decreasing costs.
- Drive down the costs of key business processes through automation.

Chief financial officers can both relate to and appreciate these types of objectives. The service provider will now be focused on achieving these objectives with the minimum of expenditure in order to maximise their profit. This promotes an "adequate at best" performance.

The big challenge is in weaving innovation into a commercial relationship. Innovation goes hand in hand with risk, and risk is the enemy of the contract. When the service is delivered internally, the CIO is likely to avoid risk because she is not remunerated on taking chances.

Service-level agreements thus appear to be "passion dampeners" in respect of what IT could potentially deliver to the business. Service level agreements in their current form reinforce the link between IT and mundane cost-cutting, which in turn reinforces the view that strategically IT doesn't really matter as it offers no real competitive advantage.

Users have low expectations

It would appear that buyer rights do not exist when it comes to IT-related products and services. When one buys a fridge or a car, one expects it to work by default and fail by exception. The converse seems to be the case in respect of IT purchases. In much the same way as a frog can be boiled if the water is heated slowly enough, the IT industry over the years has conditioned users to be braced for substandard and incident-rich delivery. It is not surprising that some users have the view that the union of IT and good service is nothing more than a fanciful romantic notion.

Similarly, from the IT department's perspective this notion is akin to focusing on the relishes when the barbeque equipment still does not work. The good news is that it will not take much to impress users in respect of IT service. The trick is upping the service levels from where they are currently and then being consistent.

The IT industry is inconsistent

The IT industry's youthful vigour makes it an exciting (and sometimes too exciting) place to work. The downside is that there is a lack of standards, or in fact sometimes the opposite is true – too many standards. This includes naming conventions in terms of IT roles (what exactly is a project manager and do they or don't they have financial responsibilities?) and the terminology (where several words mean the same thing, and a given word means different things to different people). So those who choose to work in or around IT-land are faced with learning a language that has yet to be properly documented. Worse still, perhaps, is that different IT people will give you different reasons for a given problem. Though in fairness to helpdesks, according to some users, they are at least consistent in that whatever the problem they will recommend that you reboot the system.

Beyond the helpdesk, when users ask the technologists why the system does not work they get an answer that is not always understandable to users. Oddly, when the operations manager then asks the technical architect they get a different answer. And the CEO gets yet a different answer when he liaises with the CIO. The answers may in fact be the same (though often they are not), and so there is consistency there, but the way they are expressed is inconsistent, and this arouses suspicion in the user community.

Problem Summary

Information technology leaders and the board, along with users, have responsibilities in ensuring that the IT service levels in the organisation lie somewhere between acceptable and outstanding. Thus all parties have a role to play in IT service management.

As mentioned previously, there are plenty of shrink-wrapped service management methods available, and some of them are battlefield-tested. But again a service attitude is needed to underpin the use of the associated service tools. Some industries are known for their lack of customer orientation. The building industry comes to mind. Competent technicians such as carpenters and plumbers do what they need to do, but walk away leaving a mess. Their skill is undermined by the customer's perceived experience as they endeavour to get the grit and wood shavings out of the carpet.

The reconciliation of tightly defined service levels, woven into a chaotic business environment, adds to the challenge. The boardroom's variable risk appetite, driven by near real-time bear/bull mindset flips, is akin to a luxury hotel endeavouring to meet the random needs of a schizophrenic guest. Information technology value management is seriously undermined by substandard service, regardless of whether it is actual or perceived.

Towards Service Management

Better IT service management equates to better service. A better service will certainly improve the perceived value of the IT investment in the eyes of the users, and most likely deliver better value in the eyes of the shareholders. What is certain is that bad service will undermine good relations across the IT–business divide, and that is bad for business.

This section looks at ways to improve IT service delivery.

A helpful helpdesk

Ninety per cent of user problems are trivial, so there is no need to have heavyweight technologists sitting on the helpdesk. Such "help"desk staff have been known to tell the users that they are too stupid to be using a computer. Such unsolicited advice does nothing to harmonise business–IT relationships. So, IT department helpdesks are rightly staffed by socially skilled technology "lightweights". These people determine the user experience and therefore the perception of the service. They are thus critical to good user–IT relationships.

Advising the users to reboot (or even just boot) their PCs solves most problems. Many users joke that the helpdesk could be replaced by a continuously looping telephone voice mail that simply announces the phrase "reboot your computer". The helpdesk needs to provide a more consultative service, even though the core service is "reboot your PC". With a bit more education the helpdesk can provide such a service. General practitioners in the medical industry come to mind (see Table 7.1). They can often diagnose what is wrong with the person within seconds. In the case of some neural illnesses they can diagnose the condition from hearing the person's footsteps before they come into the surgery. Despite that they give the person attention/time

Table 7.1 Impact of bedside manner on patient

Medical knowledge	Bedside manner	User perception
Excellent	Poor	Bad doctor
Average	Good	Good doctor

so they feel that they have received a good service. In essence, developing the helpdesk staff to have a better bedside manner will pay dividends in terms of user perception of IT value.

Also, some users are genuinely interested in what the error messages actually mean. So those helpdesk staff that can provide a "digital coaching" role by explaining what the associated IT buzzwords mean in non-technical language will be very much in demand.

Agree service levels

Rather than impose service levels on the IT department or assume that they will telepathically work out what the business needs, sit down and agree them. Service level definitions should take the form of a negotiation rather than an ambush. This is an opportunity for the IT department to set expectation levels, the lack of which leads to much user frustration. The challenge is to provide service levels that go beyond the "adequate is enough" bare minimum delivery to an efficient service that allows room for innovation. The traditional fixed-priced paradigm makes this difficult to do.

Businesses are encouraged to limit the fixed-price element to the more predictable deliverables such as new systems and reliable infrastructure. Beyond that, a discretionary budget should be available so that the IT department can experiment with new technologies to establish whether they will have a positive business impact – i.e., give your organisation a

competitive edge. Having put together a business case for this experimentation, the IT department submits a request to proceed. Based on
the business's risk appetite and the robustness of the business case, it will
decide whether it would like the IT department to embark on the
experimentation.

Postmodern CIOs who have developed very high trust levels with their
boardroom colleagues might explore dropping the whole fixed-price approach,
given its emphasis on passing risk to the supplier. To give the business a
sense of empowerment despite the move away from the fixed-price hand-
cuffs, the CIO might set up a triage unit managed by a board made up of
business representatives that prioritise where the IT department focuses its
energies at any point in time – possibly creating some prioritisation formula
based on a number of relevant variables including business impact.

Empower users

Ignorant customers are rarely good customers. Their lack of knowledge
tends to make them overly suspicious of the supplier, and this generates a
communication barrier that eventually leads to poor service. Educating the
users is a worthwhile investment. This could take the form of an explan-
ation of IT terminology. In general it is best not to make this the job of the
typical technologist, who may find the users' ignorance an irritation. Equally
likely is that whilst technologists can do technology they cannot necessarily
articulate what it is and how it works in layperson's terms. Fortunately for
me this has created a business opportunity in helping business people
understand IT. My aim is to help every business person become competent
in respect of IT and its impact on business.

Another approach is to hold open days, where users are invited into the IT
department to meet the technologists and the technology. Humanising the
IT department is one step towards better relations. So is providing demon-

strations of the latest funky technology. Webinars and podcasts are also increasingly popular education channels.

Create a service-oriented IT department

Technology tools are becoming more business-oriented. For example, there are business process management (BPM) tools that map business processes onto the underlying technology modules. Such tools provide the traceability needed to accelerate the detection, isolation and repair of the technology (or line of code) that underpins a "broken" process. It also forces technologists to think in terms of business processes rather than technology modules. An approach called services oriented architecture (SOA) similarly encourages this type of thinking. Ask your CIO or a marketing executive from any software company.

There is no reason why the IT department cannot be structured to map onto the business processes. This similarly will help traceability and will also help in the allocation of budget, given that some business processes are more critical than others.

Appoint service level butlers

The use of service-level managers to ensure the IT department meets the needs of the business is not a new phenomenon, though it is far from ubiquitous. Usually, this customer-oriented interaction takes place at the line of business or department level. I advocate that the concept is extended down to the user level. I want somebody to take responsibility for the IT service I receive.

Smart service providers, having secured a contract, will focus their energies in ensuring that the users are happy. This means providing them with a stable, responsive and secure IT environment. Once that is in place the service provider will have relatively little to do, as the users now perceive the service level contract as an insurance policy against subsequent failure. They are relatively happy to continue paying for the service even though they do not appear to be getting much attention from the provider. Similarly the service level butler, in conjunction with the IT department, will invest time up front to make the user feel comfortable in respect of their IT requirements. Once achieved, the role of butler becomes less labour-intensive.

The relationship between user and butler could be strengthened by providing the latter with a bonus based on the performance of the former. The race would be on to team up with the company's high performers. Such tension would turn a languishing IT department into a Darwinian ecosystem.

Systemise innovation

Weave innovation into the agreement. Traditional service-level agreements do not encourage innovation. The fixed-price paradigm forces suppliers, whether they be internal or external, into cutting corners in order to reduce costs. Anything that actually promotes risk will be avoided. Specifying that the supplier needs to invest a certain fraction of the contract value into researching how new technologies can be used specifically to benefit the business is recommended.

Failure is to be encouraged. And the faster the failure can take place the better. In fact, the supplier should be rewarded for failure, to encourage experimentation. It is only through experimentation that innovation is uncovered. And of course some of the innovations may happen as a side-effect of the experiment; Post-it notes and Viagra come to mind.

This goes against the grain in a traditional command-and-control management structure. It will require a change in management philosophy if the

IT department is to deliver value beyond simply automating the business processes.

Reward overperformance

Avoid an "adequate is enough" mindset in the IT department by allowing them to share in the spoils of business success. IT does have a role to play in company performance, so it seems only fair. The question is how to implement a fair reward model. If we take the butler model, then the bonus should reflect how that individual has helped their associated users. The users could be given guidelines on what percentage of their remuneration/bonus they should allocate to their IT butler. Good payers would attract the best butlers, and vice versa.

Ultimately, good commercially oriented IT people will gravitate towards high-paying industries, and high-earning users in those industries. This is of course a management nightmare. But encouraging an informal model of reward over and above the commercially agreed service levels could well incentivise the top technologists and users to seek each other out. People very rarely "buy" the hair salon, they buy the hairdresser. Their loyalty is with the person they trust. In a sensitive service like IT, the hairdressing model has some merit.

Change the business model

If that is not radical enough for you, try this. Why not reduce the IT department's budget to zero? The aim here is to effect a mindset shift within the IT department from public to private sector.

Many IT departments are run like a public sector organisation. They receive an annual budget and then endeavour to meet the needs of the users. But life goes on if they fail in that respect. The customer is "locked in" so there is no real need to perform. A mindset underpinned by the fact that "users are generally ungrateful and so do not deserve good service" does not help. This is a generalisation of course, but it largely threads the thinking of many IT staff no matter how business-oriented the CIO.

A more private-sector approach will either stimulate the technologists to realise that ungrateful users pay their salaries, or cause them to abandon ship and find another organisation where they can progress their own personal agendas below the radar of business scrutiny.

Technologists in IT service companies are very aware of this approach. Working on client sites they meet users. Inappropriate attitudes to the user – for example, telling them "they are an idiot" – will be picked up by the client and reported back to the supplier. The unprofessional technologist's manager will promptly deal with the problem, which may entail dispatching the guilty party to a communications skills course. The supplier organisation understands who pays the bills and deals with such service lapses promptly. Over time, technologists working for IT service companies become quite customer-centric.

So, to migrate the IT department to this service organisation model requires radical action. The first step is for the IT department to surrender its IT budget. The second step is to explain that from this point on the IT department must win business from the business. To give the IT department a fighting chance, the business must use the IT department for a set period, say two years. This gives the IT department a chance to become service-oriented, develop sales and marketing skills, and prepare itself for competing in the wider market.

Perhaps the IT department is "gifted" the IT infrastructure business for a four-year period – i.e., the infrastructure business will be put to open tender in four years' time. Similarly, after two years the IT department will be in competition with third-party service providers in respect of applications. In effect, the IT department will be given a head start but it will need to turn that into superior service otherwise it will lose some of its business in two years' time and lose its power base in four.

In terms of the pricing plan for the business, all departments will be obliged to pay a set fee, perhaps based on number of users or usage in respect of infrastructure. And for that the users receive a reliable, responsive and secure service. In respect of applications, the IT department will quote a price to the users based on the complexity of the requirement from both a business and technology perspective, and the speed of delivery required. In essence the paying customer will be the department heads and/or line of business heads. It is up to them how they spend their budget. It is up to the CIO to encourage them to spend as much as possible on IT.

This could actually be good news for the IT department. The current model puts the IT department at the mercy of the CFO, who can determine what budget the IT department receives. This is a stressful model, particularly if the CFO is cost oriented. The dotcom crash caused the CFO to decide that it was in the best interests of his company to cut IT spend. This caused the IT market to dry up. But if the decision is handed to the business heads, then they are less likely to think cost reduction. In a down market they might think people reduction, but increase IT spend.

Thus the proposed model is more likely to protect the IT department from market downturns and cost-obsessed CFOs. However, for it to work, the service delivered needs to be such that the internal customers genuinely see it as a contributor to enhanced business value. With such a model the IT department is unlikely to undertake "we know best" projects where perhaps the CIO altruistically believes the business needs another system (e.g., a data warehouse) and builds it regardless of the needs of the business. Often this is a result of technologists, who goad the CIO into "fun" projects. Such projects will at least meet their objectives of getting hands-on experience in a hot new technology and/or provide a refresh for their résumés. If nobody is paying for it then it is less likely to happen. Information technology is now fully in tune with the business objectives. Everyone gets a basic or hygiene level of IT service, but those that pay the most get the best service. The death of the IT budget, or at least its decentralisation, whilst painful in the short term, might ultimately help keep the IT department relevant in the eyes of the boardroom.

Adopt good practice

The IT industry is responding, albeit slowly, to the need for a more systematic approach to software engineering and infrastructure management. There are a number of tried-and-tested approaches in place, which are gaining traction across the industry. Most are process-oriented and a few are people-oriented. Nonetheless, the process side is a very important element in delivering a responsive and a reliable service. This market is evolving rapidly, so it is recommended that you research what is available. It may even be wise to take the best bits of each methodology to create an approach that genuinely meets your needs.

Action Summary

Good IT service management is an essential element of maximising IT value. Good service promotes trust between users and technologists, which in turn leads to greater service. Such a virtuous cycle is to be encouraged. Good practice within the IT department needs to be complemented with good customer interaction. In the extreme, the IT department should operate on an "eat what it kills" basis, so that it starts to perceive the delivery of IT services as a privilege rather than a right.

Service Management – External Perspectives

This section provides an alternative view to my own in respect of service management. The contributors were asked to answer one or more of the following questions:

- Why is service management important?
- Why is this not generally being addressed?
- What are the underlying problems?
- What are the consequences of failing to address this issue?
- What advice would you give in respect of service management?

Why is service management important?

> The IT service proposition is the building block for creating trust between IT and its customers. Many IT departments and CIOs do not understand the criticality of this foundation and are unable to therefore drive change or have a seat at the CEO table. The users are constantly comparing their systems and application services to their best of breed experiences in their daily life. They equate their email services to the email services provided by the Yahoos and the MSNs and if IT cannot deliver the minimum service level, the business perception of IT gets tainted and it becomes difficult to conduct open and honest discussions on critical and strategic matters.
>
> ***Rumi Contractor, CIO, HSBC Europe***

> Developing a service mentality is good for those organisations that feel that IT is an overhead that falls into "fixed costs".
>
> ***Karen Mellor, IT Capability Associate Director, Astra Zeneca***

The trust levels between the users and the IT department will be determined by the quality of the service. Poor trust levels will impact the value one receives from the IT investment.

Rob Fraser, IT Director, Alliance Boots

As a senior IT manager of Deloitte's in Ireland I am responsible for ensuring that the IT infrastructure supports both our consultants and our management. As a business, we are people-focused, but we are underpinned by IT. IT failures will very likely have direct consequences for our clients. Thus the service we provide is critical to Deloitte's reputation management.

Goretti McCormack-George, Senior IT Manager, Deloitte

The business and the IT department usually have one thing in common – they work for the same ultimate employer. The best IT departments are recognised as providing a service. They have developed "trust and reliability in delivery" with their customers – the business – with people relationships strongly influenced by their allegiance to the same employer. If the business sees the IT department as an overhead that is not delivering business benefit then it will be rationalised and probably outsourced.

Steve Tyler, UK Programmes Director, LogicaCMG

This needs to be taken seriously so you can then have the discussions that really matter – the ones about business transformation with technology. There is a danger that IT departments can be so focused on service delivery in a narrow sense (helpdesk average time to answer, time to close calls, etc.) that they lose focus on the important things such as how to actually make the business run more efficiently, identify new opportunities, reduce risks and grow.

Nick Leake, Director of Operations and Infrastructure, ITV

Why is this not generally being addressed?

CIOs by nature want to do the next big thing or make a big impact and as such find service management mundane and boring. In my opinion, the CIO who does not have an appreciation of the ground realities is incapable of setting and leading strategic changes or transformation and as such is bound to meet resistance or fail trying.

Rumi Contractor, CIO, HSBC Europe

Some organisations do not necessarily perceive what the IT department delivers as a service. And so do not think in terms of service quality.

Rob Fraser, IT Director, Alliance Boots

In my view many IT departments fail to deliver a quality service to their users because of either a lack of service standards or a rigid adherence to service level agreements. The day-to-day pressures of operational delivery can lead to either of these extremes.

Goretti McCormack-George, Senior IT Manager, Deloitte

"Service" implies more interaction with business people and many IT departments are still dominated by highly technical people who find it difficult to communicate and interact easily with their business user colleagues. Embracing a "service" culture and the associated changes in behaviour and approach does not come naturally and must often be seeded by an active campaign of education and business change.

Steve Tyler, UK Programmes Director, LogicaCMG

It is hard to define what the services are. IT services are not naturally defined in a language people understand. Nor is it consistent from one organisation to another. Things like ITIL and CMM provide a framework that helps with service definition, but you still have to identify and define services with users. Frankly this is tedious and it is often hard to see the associated value.

Nick Leake, Director of Operations and Infrastructure, ITV

Many IT departments see themselves as leading change rather than partnering or servicing change. There is a feeling that the change-experts reside within IT and that it's the technology that causes the change. This causes friction.

Karen Mellor, IT Capability Associate Director, Astra Zeneca

What are the underlying problems?

A neglected relationship with a strategic supplier may lead to the service you have signed up for in respect of IT delivery no longer meeting the needs of the business, particularly if the business has either just moved into or out of a period of transformation.

Rob Fraser, IT Director, Alliance Boots

Most of the service management issues stem from years of neglect or years of fast-paced but half-cooked implementations. The net impact to an organisation is that of a bloated, unhealthy plethora of systems, bespoke and in many cases badly configured applications without any end-to-end transactional monitoring, resulting in unnecessary costs, complication and highly unstable and very difficult to maintain services. Changes become time-consuming and any change activity creates an opportunity for failure and outages while adding to the ever-increasing complexity.

The work of the IT associates becomes a nightmare causing reputational damage both to the organisation and IT in particular, further eroding the "trust" and influence of IT and the CIO.

Rumi Contractor, CIO, HSBC Europe

Presenting value or convincing the business of value can be a difficult task. If a system is shown to break a constraint for the business, then its value needs to be made apparent and convincing.

High quality connectivity from "anytime, anywhere" is expected – but ubiquity and consistency is still not the norm, this is regularly seen as an IT problem. Explaining the limits of a technology and understanding the key requirements can go a long way to setting realistic expectations.

Critical information is transferred across many systems, stored and reused creating risks from lack of version and document management control. However, IT is often left to answer the business question without proper understanding of the problems.

Goretti McCormack-George, Senior IT Manager, Deloitte

Technology doesn't lead the change; it supports it. This concept needs to be shared by customers and service providers in IT. A more customer-centric approach is required.

Karen Mellor, IT Capability Associate Director, Astra Zeneca

Getting the correct KPIs in place that the business can relate to, i.e., meaningful ones. Some implement KPIs, with the objective of micro management, which prove nothing.

Vivian Ash, Group Information Manager, BASF

There remain real-world problems in creating services understood by the business. IT organisations sometimes feel they have done the service job by creating, monitoring (Service Level Agreements) and charging for the "mainframe service" or "networks service". Unfortunately these are not services the business can understand, influence or control. Building business-oriented services is far more complex, as these services require both an abstraction and an integration of the technology services. For example, in retail banking, a "customer account management" service might consist of several back-end systems, multiple hardware and communication platforms and three or four front-end customer interface systems. Working out the overall quality of service and cost (perhaps even to the cost per transaction) is very challenging. Notwithstanding the claims of systems management tool vendors, building such a mechanism is a major undertaking and beyond the capabilities of many IT organisations.

Richard Boreham, IT Strategy, Governance and Performance Practice Leader, KPMG

The sheer complexity of technology. Plus trying to represent it in terms of user-friendly services.

Nick Leake, Director of Operations and Infrastructure, ITV

What are the consequences of failing to address this issue?

Mismatch of expectations in business areas and IT.

Karen Mellor, IT Capability Associate Director, Astra Zeneca

Without a voice at the table, the CIO is unable to drive change or influence business strategies or desires.

Rumi Contractor, CIO, HSBC Europe

A disenchanted team that is seen as being neither reactive nor proactive in the eyes of the business. Usually because the IT department fails to understand that they are a service and the business is their customer.

Vivian Ash, Group Information Manager, BASF

In a business like Deloitte's, the immediate impact of poor IT service management is a diminished customer experience. Where IT failures impact regulatory compliance the consequences for all concerned are dire.

Goretti McCormack-George, Senior IT Manager, Deloitte

An outsourcer may be brought in who does this resulting in a large cost of "transition" as all the services are defined. But ultimately if users feel they are getting a good service it will be irrespective of who delivers or what the statistics say.

Nick Leake, Director of Operations and Infrastructure, ITV

What advice would you give in respect of addressing this issue?

Be prepared to redefine the boundaries of responsibility when the IT department has outsourced some of its service deliver to a third party. Users tend to have unreasonably high expectations of the third-party supplier. This can put unnecessary stress on the supplier, which can ultimately lead to a breakdown in service. It will help if the IT department retains critical control points in the service delivery so that the users have more reasonable expectations.

Rob Fraser, IT Director, Alliance Boots

The CIO needs to ensure that the foundation of the IT department is secure. This must not be a periodic event or activity. One needs to constantly and consistently focus on service management to ensure that the environment is simple, automated, and the organisation is able to deliver on promises made.

Rumi Contractor, CIO, HSBC Europe

Work on a service catalogue. Get the base line right. Deliver the expected service and make it visible. Keep costs to the minimum by only funding agreed work and ensuring the portfolio is prioritised and agreed by business stakeholders. Earn the confidence then move into the partnership phase (and also maverick phase with high potential projects) with revenue ring fenced for innovation.

Karen Mellor, IT Capability Associate Director, Astra Zeneca

I would encourage IT departments to adopt a genuine customer service ethic. Those that work in the IT department should be appraised on their customer-centricity. Those that lack a service ethic should be moved away from the customer interface and ideally away from the company.

Goretti McCormack-George, Senior IT Manager, Deloitte

There is a danger that a subservient service provider may not be best positioned to engage as a business transformation partner.

Nick Leake, Director of Operations and Infrastructure, ITV

CIRCULATION
MANAGEMENT

"It is not enough to have knowledge, one must also apply it."

Johann von Goethe, German Playwright

In this chapter:

- The need for circulation management.
- Circulation management – why it doesn't happen.
- Towards circulation management.
- Circulation management – external perspectives.

value management

circulation management

service management

technology management

people entwinement

process entwinement

strategy entwinement

The Need for Circulation Management

I have struggled to come up with a better term for this layer of the IT Value Stack. The term "circulation" is a reference to the flow of data, information, knowledge and ultimately wisdom around the organisation. Management of this "stuff" is important if the organisation is to reap best value from its IT systems. Having the best hardware and software counts for nothing if the users do not get the data . . . wisdom they need, when and where they need it.

Good circulation management also underpins good governance. This in itself should be sufficient reason to pay attention to this layer of the IT Value Stack.

Some definitions

Terms like data and information are used interchangeably, but there is a difference. So let's look at those terms associated with the lifeblood of an organisation, namely:

- **Data**
  - Raw facts and figures.
  - For example, a stack of candidate résumés.
- **Information**
  - Processed facts and figures.
  - For example, the number of new technology candidates living in Moscow.
- **Knowledge**
  - 'Considered' information.
  - For example, knowing that this is much higher than anywhere else in the world.

- **Wisdom**
  - Acting on knowledge.
  - For example, deciding to relocate there given this knowledge.

Not everyone will agree on these definitions, but at least they give a sense of the relative importance of the lifeblood constituents.

The knowledge challenge

Data and information management are relatively mature practices. Information technology provides a key link between data and information. In essence, IT systems convert data into information. A mistake made in the late twentieth century was to similarly regard knowledge management as a technology issue. Technology does indeed play a part in the delivery of knowledge, but more often than not the knowledge is stored in the heads of the employees. Many organisations attempt to institutionalise that knowledge by ordering their staff to deposit their knowledge into, for example, the customer database, or to produce a white paper that can be shared with fellow staff.

Smart employees know that in modern-day business the currency of value is knowledge. So it would be foolish to surrender it. Better to maximise the return on the knowledge by trading it. This often happens during both job interviews and performance reviews.

Smart employers recognise this and create an environment that effectively rewards knowledge-sharing. So it is somewhat irritating that you find yourself having to buy the knowledge from the employee despite the fact that you have in many cases paid them to acquire it.

Knowledge management, which might better be called knowledge-sharing management, does require collaborative technologies such as workflow and groupware applications. The smart deployment of such technologies has the potential to optimise the circulation of knowledge in your organisation, which consequently improves the value extracted from the IT investment.

The wisdom vision

Most organisations are still focused on information management, never mind knowledge management. So, many will consider talk of wisdom management as science fiction or just a romantic notion. I believe that in time, knowledge will become a commodity – so it will not be enough just to know, for example, that the market is about to flip. Everyone will eventually be in a position to predict the future, to some extent – those who know what to do with that knowledge will have the competitive advantage.

So, in a post-knowledge economy, organisations will stock their intellectual capital with wisdom rather than knowledge. Wisdom comes from experience. But there is nothing to stop a teenager from becoming wise should he decide to study the teachings of the great thinkers over the last 3000 years, and then – most importantly – apply that wisdom to real-world situations. Thus the teenager has short-circuited the "speed to wisdom" path, and so does not have to wait until he is grey haired before gaining his wisdom stripes.

Similarly, organisations can accelerate their wisdom acquisition by capitalising on the experiences, both good and bad, of other organisations and individuals. Not dissimilar to case-based reasoning, as used in legal decision-making, organisations will be able to buy packaged wisdom and through the use of intelligent tools apply this wisdom to address their business challenges.

But it is perhaps premature to talk about wisdom management. Perhaps regard its consideration as a hedge bet against the possibility that there won't be a nuclear Armageddon that resets the industrial clock back to agricultural or an even earlier era – though if you can start applying the principles today, you are likely to get even more value from your IT investment in the future.

Governance

Corporate governance is a hot topic at board level and will continue to be so, probably for ever. The need to manage your organisation's key assets responsibly is being "encouraged" by the raft of regulatory compliance legislation belching from every direction. Assets include people, technology, intellectual property and your capital. Whilst all need to be managed with care, the capital and in particular financial accounting is attracting much of the governance spotlight. Worldcom, Parmalat and Enron have all played a part in setting new standards in respect of corporate governance.

It is not enough to adopt best governance practice. There is often a legal need to demonstrate good governance. This is generally displayed by implementing "controls" on the business processes to ensure that irregular activities are detected. These controls are (or should be) built into the IT systems that underpin the business processes. Thus, your corporate governance framework is only as good as the associated IT systems. Poor IT systems can lead to imprisonment and good IT systems can protect against financial and, perhaps more seriously, reputational damage. Corporate governance has driven the emergence of IT governance. Organisations are now looking at their IT practices. Poor IT practices equate to poor corporate governance.

In any case, the IT controls will only be effective if your circulation management approach ensures that these controls generate the right information, and that information is delivered to those that need to know in a timely manner. Poor circulation management equates to poor governance, and the associated penalties are painful.

Being smarter

Those that circulate their corporate lifeblood most effectively are most likely to have the best-informed staff. The best-informed staff are likely to make the smartest decisions. The organisations that make the smartest decisions prosper. This is a simple argument for investing in circulation technologies, and for managing this element of the IT Value Stack carefully. The IT department understands this but needs strong direction on what is to be available to whom, when and where. In the absence of this guidance, the IT department is likely to make some uninformed and potentially expensive decisions.

Hunt as a pack

Many organisations are:

- Repeating mistakes daily.
- Failing to exploit what they know.
- Punching below their weight.

A lack of circulation management results in the organisation failing to learn from its mistakes and successes. This is costly, and results in big organisations becoming disadvantaged rather than empowered by their size. This is, of course, great news for smaller competing organisations.

Geographically distributed organisations with multiple lines of business have the most to gain by hunting as a pack rather than as a loose federation, where the only commonality is the holding company. Once they get their act together on the circulation front, the smaller companies will lose their lack of disadvantage (aka advantage) in comparison with their larger competitors. Good circulation is a strategic initiative to ensure that your organisation has a chance of being a consumer rather than a consumee in your industry's Pac-Man tournament.

Institutionalising what your staff know

There is a direct correlation between the knowledge of your people and the value of your organisation. One day this intellectual capital will be a standard entry in company accounts. However, having knowledgeable staff is not enough. Only knowledge that is institutionalised – i.e., under the control of the organisation – can be considered as a company asset. I touched on the fact that some staff, most notably those in sales, are loath to share their knowledge unless incentivised to do so. This needs to be addressed, otherwise your share price is likely to drop every time key staff leave the office (unless of course you can convince the market that they will be returning again the next morning, and every working morning thereafter). Once the knowledge is institutionalised, your organisation, through good circulation management, can ensure that it is made available to those that need to know in a timely manner. A failure on this front will lead to knowledge being used for internal power plays rather than in the best interests of the shareholders.

Get real

There is much talk about the real-time organisation. Such organisations are sometimes referred to as on-demand, adaptive and even Darwinian. The underlying belief is that those organisations that adapt best to the ever-changing environment will survive. Organisations that intend to become more responsive to the market need to ensure that their market sensors are in place and are set to sensitive. These sensors can be either digital (your market-facing IT systems) or organic (your market-facing staff). Ensuring that both types of sensors relay what they detect to those that can act on the information is critical.

A classic example is the chain that links sales staff to IT staff via product and marketing staff. This chain exists where the organisation is selling an IT-centric product or service, for example online corporate banking. How many great product enhancement ideas are captured by the sales staff but fail to get to the IT department for implementation because there was no knowledge supply chain in place to formally capture and process the valuable nuggets of intelligence that are hitting the business every day. Like meteors hitting the Earth's atmosphere, most ideas are vaporised on entry into the organisation. To continue with the astrophysical analogy, it is equally important that your knowledge supply chain vaporises many of the less than useful ideas before they damage your organisation. So in essence your knowledge supply chain needs to filter out bad ideas and keep track of good ones.

To switch to a medical analogy, if we regard the data through to wisdom as the lifeblood of an organisation, then we need to have the veins (business processes/IT systems) in place to handle lifeblood delivery to those that need it. These veins need to be cholesterol-free to ensure that the circulation supports the real-time functioning of the corporate organism.

The role of email

Email is much used but is little understood from a circulation perspective. It is a powerful tool, but like most powerful tools it can become dangerous in the hands of untrained users. Some might say that email is a type of virus that consumes storage media. One email can multiply thanks to the "cc" function. Less socially skilled people like to hide behind text rather than have a conversation with the person sitting opposite them.

Email has a crucial role to play in circulation management and so needs to be managed. Those that do this successfully today will gain competitive advantage. Those that don't even bother to do it tomorrow should expect to be competitively disadvantaged.

Rationale Summary

Smart organisations will make better and more timely business decisions through good circulation management. Circulation management ultimately keeps directors out of prison; free-flowing lifeblood underpins good governance. At the very least organisations will fail to yield the full value of their IT investment if they have not addressed the circulation of their data, information and knowledge. Information technology value optimisation and good governance are two reasons to pay attention to circulation management.

Circulation Management – Why it Doesn't Happen

There is circulation of data, information, knowledge and wisdom (lifeblood) in most organisations. But the circulation channels are often blocked or clogged up. As a result, those that rely on the lifeblood underperform and in some cases, much like frostbite, whither and die (literally in the healthcare and defence sectors).

This section looks at some of the main causes of poor circulation.

A weak heart

Good circulation needs a good pump. The IT department thus has to take charge of the inflow and outflow of the corporate lifeblood. To some extent it must perform the job of the liver and kidneys by purifying the inputs before pumping the aggregated output back out to those that need it. Because many organisations do not think in terms of lifeblood flow, preferring to think in terms of processing, there is no central function to gather, purify, enrich and dispatch the lifeblood.

Organisations that have grown by acquisition are in danger of having multiple hearts beating asynchronously in different parts of the body. Consequently there is a danger of inconsistent information. For example, some systems may provide end-of-day data and some may provide real-time data. If I bank with an organisation that provides some of my data in real time and the rest "end of day", I can never be sure how accurate the information is regarding my account balance. Scale this up to a corporate client with multiple accounts dealing in multiple currencies across different geographies and you can see the headaches facing the group treasurer.

Clogged arteries

High quality lifeblood will not deliver business value if the route it takes from source to where it is needed is littered with obstacles, by which I mean:

- Poor processes.
- An overreliance on human intervention.
- Political barriers.

This takes us back to process entwinement, which sits at level 2 of the IT Value Stack. But it also involves people entwinement (level 3).

The IT department typically cannot influence many of the artery-clogging issues that impact the flow of lifeblood to the users and therefore cannot be held responsible for the associated circulation problems. Until senior executives recognise this, the IT investment will continue to underperform.

As the users become increasingly dependent on the lifeblood for making critical decisions, an inefficient supply chain will result in corrupted intelligence. The armed forces have been aware of this for many years. It is time for the commercial sector to take this on board.

Political barriers

Where there are humans there is politics, which can be somewhat value-sapping. The most successful businesses in a mature market are those that can do it cheapest, and that includes innovation. At that point humans become an expensive luxury, unless they "touch" the customer or work in the IT department. Some may see the arguments between two divisional heads as childlike behaviour; both vying for the attention (and ultimately the position) of the CEO. Shareholders may see this as corporate inefficiency.

Such political activity creates barriers to the circulation of corporate lifeblood. Divisional heads sometimes forget that business is a team sport, and their sister divisions are on the same side. Hoarding of market intelligence, for example, results in underutilisation of the company's intellectual assets. This problem is particularly rife amongst acquisitive organisations that are now faced with multiple cultures and a federalist management structure. An acid test to detect whether a company suffers from this problem is to establish how many CRM (customer relationship management) systems they have. Answers greater than one should ring alarm bells.

Poor data management

Let us look at data, which is the most fundamental lifeblood constituent to be circulated around the organisation. Data management covers:

Data acquisition. This is the process of gathering data via other systems, files and people. Think GIGO (Garbage In Garbage Out). Sloppy data entry with poor data validation ultimately leads to poor business decisions.

Data cleansing. This is a variation on data acquisition most closely associated with data warehousing, where the data are transferred from a number of operational databases to one repository. The benefit of this is that users can analyse the consolidated data more easily. The process of transferring data from multiple databases into one invariably requires the data to be "scrubbed", so that it is stored in a consistent format. For example, Male/Female are stored as either M/F or Male/Female and not some combination of these.

Data storage. The building of databases suitable for the storage of the data required by the business is key to good data storage. Poorly designed databases with unnecessary duplication of data are a source of problems. How many different ways does your bank spell your name? It is in rough proportion to the number of services you use. The trouble is that your data is held in multiple service-silo databases that are not integrated together. So the bank does not see your full value and treats you accordingly.

Often, database developers mistakenly presume what the business needs by way of data, and this has the effect of reducing the value of the data held.

Data dispersal. This involves the delivery of data from the database to the users and adjoining systems. Poor querying tools reduce the effectiveness of the data from a user's perspective. Inconsistent data formats across the organisation lead to problems, particularly when data replication is required across different systems. In a perfect world, within an organisation, or even within a sector, date (for example) would be stored in a form such as dd/mm/yy or mm/dd/yyyy, but not both.

These issues have plagued organisations for several decades. Despite being a theme of the 1970s, data management is still not a refined science. This is a problem.

Poor information management

Information management became the theme of the 1980s, though the tools used to turn data into information continue to evolve today. In fact, these so-called BI (business intelligence) tools are becoming more important to information management than the databases onto which they are bolted.

Big companies have the biggest problems in respect of information management. With their databases distributed across many buildings, functions and geographies, they have a real challenge understanding such issues as "who are our top 10 customers globally?" or establishing "whether there is a correlation between the number of nappies and volume of beer sold in our out of town supermarkets?" The ability to make intelligent business decisions through the use of information gleaned from one's data warehouse is in part down to the quality of the tools, which are generally very good. And in part down to the design of the underpinning data repositories and the quality of the data they receive, which are not always so good. The fact that many companies do not know what their information requirements are adds to the problem.

In the absence of user guidance, the IT department has to guess what is required, and this invariably is not quite what the users want. And even if the users are crystal clear on their data/information requirements, there is still the risk that they may misinterpret their subsequent data mining forays and so make potentially disastrous business decisions.

Enterprise applications from vendors provide the ideal set-up to gather and consolidate the corporation's data such that users receive accurate information. But many organisations are concerned about committing to one vendor and so have a variety of enterprise applications, which were never designed to work together. This approach avoids vendor lock-in but impairs the quality of the associated information.

Generally speaking, information management is problematic. The IT department has less control over this than perhaps the business expects. The abdication of information management responsibility by the business to the IT department is a significant cause of poor lifeblood circulation. Not unlike decoupling the brain from the heart.

Non-existent knowledge management

Knowledge management fundamentals include being able to communicate with everyone in the business by phone and email. But some organisations fail these entry conditions, particularly with the absence of a corporate phone directory and a variety of incompatible and sometimes decoupled email systems. Barriers to communication are barriers to good knowledge management.

Next level up is moving beyond "white pages" directories containing the contact details of all staff to having a "yellow pages" that includes the expertise of all the staff categorised in a search-friendly manner. The acid test is how easily you can establish who in your organisation is expert at writing sales proposals, advising on e-business law or Mexican trade unions. The examples may not map onto your business, but many organisations don't have their information centralised (or more appropriately classified), and thus don't consequently know what the organisation (or more specifically its staff) is good at. This leads to a tremendous underutilisation of one's intellectual assets, which today is careless and tomorrow will result in boardroom dismissal for poor use of company resources.

The use of collaborative tools such as workflow and groupware technologies builds upon knowing who is good at what, but as your organisation's community extends further along the supplier and customer chains, the boundary that defines your business (and defines the protective fence that surrounds your knowledge capital) starts to blur. Good knowledge management has the power to really deliver excellent business value. But technology only plays a bit-part; people are the stars of the show. Getting them to play ball is a cultural challenge for many organisations. The IT department could play a role in selling the concept of knowledge management and the associated technologies to the users, but few businesses see this as a job for the CIO.

Too much email

At one extreme email can be seen as a virus that eats valuable company resources on arrival, both in terms of storage and time. Poorly written and insensitive emails can also inadvertently damage relationships and so undermine circulation. Another less well documented, but perhaps more worrying, aspect of email is how important it is in the role of inter-process communication (IPC). Whilst many business processes are automated, the links between these processes are often semi-automated. That is to say, IT is used to circulate data between processes but is often dependent on a human making this happen. Typically the output of one process is delivered to the next process via email. For example, a new employee is added to the personnel system via the HR department. The HR department then alerts the payroll department to include the new starter on the payroll, usually via email. Humans being humans may forget to send the email or mistype the salary figure. This is of course irritating for the new starter, unless the salary is more than agreed. From a business perspective semi-antomated IPCs are very inefficient and error-prone. Reliance on humans and emails to bind your critical business processes together is a problem.

Modern enterprise applications automate the links between business processes, and so are not reliant on human-induced email. However, many organisations do not have end-to-end enterprise applications and so the risk remains.

Poor document process automation

Most organisations circulate at least some of their data via paper. The circulation of paper may be internal (e.g., pay slip distribution) or it may be external (e.g., invoices, Dunning letters or bank statements). There are great savings to be made in automating one's document-related processes. But as a science, Document Process Automation appears to be in its infancy. There is a slow movement towards electronic bill/invoice presentment and payment. But even where paper is still used, there are inefficiencies in the production process. Administrative staff constructing and labelling letters individually is a sign of great inefficiency.

Banks and utility companies have seen the benefits of document process automation. Those that continue to generate paper using human-intensive business processes are still quite some way from extracting best value from their use of IT.

Poor organisational structures

Information technology cannot in itself guarantee good circulation. Today people still play a significant role in the circulation and utilisation of the corporate lifeblood. People tend to communicate badly or at least with reticence to those they don't know or trust. The ideal conditions for lack of trust are when a company is not really a company but a loose federation of companies. Some organisations that have grown rapidly by acquisition have overlooked the need for cultural integration. The acquired organisation's senior management can sometimes take a General Custer approach to their operational activities, seeing the acquiring organisation as the enemy. So, seamless IT systems that link the various entities together will be ineffective. This is a people issue.

But even if everyone is delighted "post mergers and acquisitions" there is still the issue of entwining business processes and ensuring that data is stored consistently across the newly enlarged organisation. This is an issue that again is not within the control of the IT department, though the ramifications of the associated problems will often be left at the IT department's doorstep. Ultimately, poor circulation across loosely federated organisations will lead to poor business decisions, which will eventually lead to the dismantling or decay of the organisation.

Problem Summary

There are many obstacles to good circulation management. Many of these lie beyond the control of the IT department. For this reason it would be unfair to expect the IT department to carry the full burden of delivering the maximum return on the organisation's investment in IT.

Much like strategy entwinement and process entwinement, circulation management is a business-wide challenge. Business leaders need to recognise this and then take charge in addressing the issues that obstruct good circulation. Failure in this respect is poor governance and will impinge on the bottom line.

Towards Circulation Management

We have established that circulation management (the efficient flow of data, information and knowledge around an organisation to the people that need it when and where they need it) has a significant role to play in leveraging best value from one's IT investment. We have also discovered that good circulation management is a responsibility that extends beyond the influence of the IT department.

This section examines what action can be taken to maximise the return on your IT investment from a circulation management perspective.

Develop an IT-centric culture

A cohesive culture is generally regarded as a good thing. Successful teams have a common esprit de corps and high mutual trust levels. But many organisations have at least two teams, and they aren't labelled A and B. They appear to live parallel lives and speak different languages. The trust levels between these two tribes are often very low. These tribes sit on either side of the business–IT department demilitarised zone.

Only when IT and business people communicate on the same wavelength will IT departments deliver the appropriate technology platforms to facilitate good circulation management.

Improve data management

Good data management provides a strong platform for good circulation. Very often nobody has responsibility for the data stored in the organisation. Appointing a data manager/architect will help to ensure that only data that are relevant to the users are captured and stored. This exercise could save large sums of money, not least in storage hardware. Perhaps old IT systems are forcing users to capture data that are no longer relevant to the business. The production of a data model that shows the data stored by the IT department could be used as the basis for establishing what data are actually required by the business. Please note that the production of the data model could become a very time-consuming activity, particularly where there have been a number of mergers and acquisitions since the last data model was produced.

Creating a set of data flow diagrams that show the movement of data through the business will help identify any inaccuracies in the data model. The resultant data model will be the blueprint from which subsequent databases can be constructed. It will also provide valuable input into your process engineering and technology strategy.

Improve information management

Investment in good business intelligence tools will enable you to extract valuable information from your data repository. At one extreme there are the simple reporting tools that, for example, list all the staff coming up to retirement. The other extreme is a 3D holographic representation of the per capita wealth of all citizens across Europe. The former would be useful for ordering retirement gifts, the latter for making a decision as to where you launch your luxury product.

These tools will, of course, provide a more accurate picture if they are underpinned by data that are both comprehensive and consistent. Generally, cross-company data are sourced from multiple operational databases. As mentioned earlier, common data may be held inconsistently across this array of databases. Redesigning the databases to be more consistent is out of the question (too expensive), so binding these together in the form of a data warehouse is the answer. This approach enables the data from the operational databases to be cleansed and deposited into one read-only database. The data-cleansing process ensures that the data entering the repository are consistent with the common formats defined. So, for example, as mentioned earlier, all data relating to gender are stored as Male/Female in the repository even though they were stored as 1/0 or M/F in some of the operational databases.

A well-designed data warehouse coupled with good business intelligence tools will yield valuable information. Poorly designed data warehouses will give users a false sense of security that could lead to disastrous business decisions. Thus undercooking the investment in this respect is unwise.

Improve knowledge management

Knowledge management involves much more than IT. Information technology driven approaches in the past have largely been unsuccessful. Ultimately it is about profitability, and in service organisations in particular, it is about people. But where the people are geographically dispersed, whether office-bound or in the field, IT has a significant role to play.

At a fundamental level everyone in the organisation needs to be able to communicate with everybody else regardless of proximity, whether that be by phone, email, video, chat or SMS. There needs to be one overarching intranet. Increasingly that needs to extend beyond the office boundaries to the field operatives.

The next level of knowledge management maturity is to identify who is expert at what and to make that information available to all. Thus a global yellow pages is required. The bigger the organisation the more critical this is. Harnessing the expertise of company experts will only take place if those that need help know whom to contact.

The next level of KM achievement is where the company "only ever makes the same mistake once". We become wise by making mistakes, particularly if we learn not to repeat them. Large organisations often repeat their mistakes because the lessons learnt are not shared with the rest of the business, or, worse still, there is no mechanism to share the lessons. Thus some sort of globally accessible case-study repository is required.

Successful knowledge management also embraces information and data management. Thus these need to be firmly under control before the full value of knowledge management can be extracted. Again the underlying IT infrastructure needs to support the identification and flow from those who have the knowledge to those who need it when they need it. In this respect IT is playing a key role in squeezing value from the organisation's intellectual capital.

Knowledge can be acquired at an organisational level by buying it in through consultants or acquiring knowledge-rich organisations. In parallel, one can enhance the knowledge of the existing workforce by encouraging a learning culture. IT plays a role here in terms of e-learning, or more specifically web-based learning. This is a controversial topic because e-learning was oversold as a concept some years ago. Its advocates promised the death of classroom training. Today e-learning does have a role alongside classroom training. The term "blended learning" has evolved – perhaps in order to help the e-learning advocates save face, since the world of learning didn't quite pan out as they had planned.

Moving towards a learning organisation that nurtures its intellectual capital from within requires infrastructural investment in IT. The good news is that the investment required is relatively small in respect of web-learning.

Information lifecycle management

Circulation management extends to accessing data in real time right through to data retrieval from the archives. The success of the former may be necessary to ensure the organisation is not exposed to unnecessary risk; think investment bank foreign exchange feeds and military weapon systems. The success of the latter keeps the regulators off your back when they demand to see the emails relating to a correspondence between two staff four years ago.

There is, as always, a trade-off. In this case it is between speed of access and cost of access. Tape storage is cheap and slow. Computer memory (RAM) is fast and expensive. ILM is "talk of the town" amongst storage vendors, the general theme being that the urgency of information (though like me they may have struggled to find a good collective term for data and information) decreases with time and so it makes sense to store it on the cheapest media possible. A good information lifecycle approach is key to good circulation management.

Automate inter-process communications

As mentioned earlier, whilst most business processes have some degree of automation through IT, many of the inter-process communications are handled manually or via email. Chains, of course, are only as strong as their weakest link. The same applies to business process flows.

There is a tendency to automate business processes using the "wares" of the enterprise application vendors. These vendors have a tendency to ensure that their software modules, which usually map very well onto standard business processes, dovetail together beautifully. Not surprisingly, they design their module interfaces to make it very difficult to interface their software with modules from rivals. If you are a major buyer of such services, I suggest you team up with other major buyers and encourage the vendor(s) to adopt a more open approach to inter-vendor connectivity.

Whether your business processes are based on packaged/customisable software or you have written your own software, the issue of inter-process communication needs to be addressed. Email and humans are generally not reliable in this respect and their involvement introduces unnecessary risk to your organisation.

Consider documentation management

Technologies that support the automation of document processing have the potential to save your organisation significant sums of money in respect of human labour, paper and postage. Documentation is often a mechanism for inter-process communication with the customer – for example, a bank statement or payment overdue letter. There is also an opportunity to drive costs out of the supply chain by automating the associated document management. Order documentation, bills of lading and letters of credit would all benefit from automation. In some cases, it will not only reduce cost but also speed up the physical transaction. This may in turn provide cash-flow advantages to either the buyer or the seller, depending on who wields the most power.

Influential buyers such as Wal-mart are always looking to shave cost off their products. This generally involves squeezing their suppliers on price. When the supplier really cannot offer further savings then the mechanism by which the buyer–supplier relationship is conducted is scrutinised for efficiency. At this point document management becomes significant. Big buyers increasingly expect smaller sellers to reduce paper flow. If paper makes up a significant aspect of the data flow media in your organisation, then document automation will deliver great savings.

Automating processes that currently have a "paper element" is a relatively easy way in which to squeeze more value from your IT investment. And being eco-friendly, it can be detailed in your corporate and social responsibility report.

Go wireless

Increasingly, users need access to the corporate data when they are out of the office. Sales people would certainly benefit from this, as would military personnel. Wireless technology has evolved rapidly in the last few years and whether the IT department likes it or not (and their concerns are understandable), wireless user devices are now part of the IT infrastructure.

Customers who are the ultimate beneficiaries of good circulation want to access services when and where it suits them, rather than in a location and at a time that suits the vendor.

The IT department should be encouraged to embrace wireless technology, despite the inherent security risk associated with rogue devices (for example, PDAs and laptops). Today, the benefits outweigh the risks.

Pull up the drains

This recommendation will not be welcomed by the CFO. We have established that circulation management is fundamental to maximising the business value gained from IT. Circulation management needs to be woven deeply into the IT infrastructure. Very few organisations have a 100 % IT-free approach to circulation management. At the same time, many organisations are in need of a circulation management overhaul. Unfortunately, this cannot be achieved by bolting on another application to the existing IT investment. This is a root-and-branch overhaul that will impact potentially every IT system in your organisation. Brace yourself for a significant investment. If you feel inclined to avoid this layer of the IT Value Stack, then remember that good circulation management is key to good governance. Your existing circulation management practices could well be hiding a corporate governance time bomb; one that could detonate during or after your tenure. Resolve this today and enjoy your future retirement.

Action Summary

Circulation management brings into sharp relief issues that some organisations face but have not properly addressed – e.g., a lack of cultural coherence emerging from a series of acquisitions. Good circulation is critical to one's health and the health of one's organisation. A lack of attention in this aspect of value optimisation will undermine the efforts expended on the lower layers of the IT Value Stack.

Like practically every other aspect of IT value optimisation, the level of effectiveness is determined by the extent to which the organisation as a whole responds to the challenge. Today, leaving circulation management to the IT department will lead to underperformance of the IT assets in terms of the value they deliver to the business. As the world becomes more IT-centric and the market becomes more efficient, the difference between business success and failure will boil down to the extent to which circulation management is addressed. Circulation management is closely related to the bottom line, and so needs your attention.

Circulation Management – External Perspectives

This section provides an alternative view to my own in respect of circulation management. The contributors were asked to answer one or more of the following questions:

- Why is circulation management important?
- Why is this not generally being addressed?
- What are the underlying problems?
- What are the consequences of failing to address this issue?
- What advice would you give in respect of circulation management?

Why is circulation management important?

> To get the right information to the right people at the right time.
>
> *Vivian Ash, Group Information Manager, BASF*

Organizations across all industries have to deal with increased regulatory demands, a fluctuating market, strong competitive pressures and the perpetual focus of "doing more with less." Too often, the biggest hurdle to profitability and market leadership is the lack of predictability, accountability and performance visibility that results from fragmented or siloed information residing in disparate databases across the company. For financial services this is particularly true and has been exacerbated by increased levels of competition, sophisticated customers and complex go-to-market mix of products and channels. A ubiquitous corporate performance management model that enables a "single version of the truth" will ultimately:

- Align these go-to-market initiatives.
- Drive strong decision-making.
- Enable forward planning.
- Enable cross-departmental collaboration.
- Provide the ability to spot and rectify issues in a timely manner.

Laurence Trigwell, Senior Financial Services
Industry Director, Cognos

Why is this not generally being addressed?

Digital dashboards invariably don't work, as the infrastructures of large companies are never co-ordinated sufficiently. Small companies can't afford the luxury. Getting one's house in order to ensure effective knowledge management is a big investment with little visible return for many years. Many businesses will not fund the innovation and development costs required.

Karen Mellor, IT Capability Associate Director, Astra Zeneca

Too many initiatives, which are put in and left with no management, feedback or control.

Vivian Ash, Group Information Manager, BASF

"Business intelligence" is premised on a vision of "all users accessing all of their data, in any way they want, to best understand what is happening, why it is happening and what needs to be done to help the organization succeed." While this paradigm is generally understood and accepted, making it a reality can be a challenge, specifically for IT staff charged with delivering BI. In a typical organization:

- Data is scattered across the company.
- Data is captured by different systems.
- Data is locked in disparate silos.
- Departments are run on different platforms that don't always work together.

- Each user or groups of users demand different views of their data that are sometimes best addressed by one solution over another.

Dealing with this complexity is simply the reality of doing business, but often it is the primary reason why companies are not realizing the full benefits of their business intelligence initiatives.

Laurence Trigwell, Senior Financial Services
Industry Director, Cognos

What are the underlying problems?

Investment and development time are too much of a call on the organization's limited resources. Most companies have an agenda of efficiency and productivity in respect of their core business. Knowledge management systems have to be sponsored by the shareholders or leadership teams to push through this mindset.

Karen Mellor, IT Capability Associate Director,
Astra Zeneca

Lack of management from the business. A case of implement and forget.

Vivian Ash, Group Information Manager, BASF

What are the consequences of failing to address this issue?

One of the fundamental issues is that the individual participants providing the separate data components have an incomplete view of the entire data picture. Contributors include:

- Department heads
- Account managers
- Channel managers
- Product line managers
- Controllers
- Directors

Conversely, the senior-level consumers of this information, such as company officers and senior executives, are left to reconcile conflicting and disparate views without any insights as to the nature of the underlying data. The information lacks consistency. Inevitably analyses and strategic discussions devolve into questions about the provenance of the underlying data. And this is unfortunate because truly strategic decisions cross boundaries. In an optimized information-rich environment, a simple query has the potential to lead to more meaningful queries that ultimately drive better performance.

Laurence Trigwell, Senior Financial Services
Industry Director, Cognos

Miscommunication and poor motivation.

Vivian Ash, Group Information Manager, BASF

What advice would you give in respect of addressing this issue?

Businesses need to develop five-year plans that engage the IT depart-ment in a more strategic manner. Select key operational develop-ments that are aligned to strategy. Brace yourself for long-term IT development lifecycles knowing that these systems will ultimately deliver competitive advantage in the end. A partnership with busi-ness leaders is key. Education on the need for management of infor-mation as key is also critical.

Karen Mellor, IT Capability Associate Director, Astra Zeneca

Owing to the divergent goals of transaction performance and complex reporting and analysis, organizations have no choice but to imple-ment enterprise information architectures that employ different data structures, schemas, and environments. For example, it is impossible to deploy a single database for a financial services organization. Any attempt to do so would generate more problems than benefits.

However, without proper alignment and consistency of data from many different sources, business intelligence efforts cannot succeed. This is an area where management information systems (MIS)/IT professionals must provide leadership. By working closely with busi-ness units and senior management to:

* Interpret and aggregate information needs.
* Create and sponsor the information strategy.
* Help to set expectations.

- Provide technology leadership.
- Devise new initiatives.
- Furnish insights into underlying data.

MIS can help organizations achieve new levels of competitiveness and efficiency.

Laurence Trigwell, Senior Financial Services
Industry Director, Cognos

VALUE MANAGEMENT

> "*A cynic is one who knows the cost of everything and the value of nothing.*"

Oscar Wilde

In this chapter:

- The need for value management.
- Value management – why it doesn't happen.
- Towards value management.
- Value management – external perspectives.

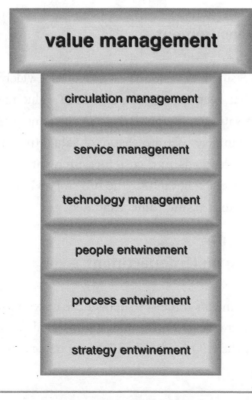

The Need for Value Management

The idea of good or better value should have universal appeal. Though having witnessed a number of market downturns, value is a concept that mistakenly gets replaced with cost during these periods, particularly when the measurement of value associated with the service in question is difficult to gauge. Information technology falls into this category, so it is necessary for CIOs to have a model for measuring value. At the very least value measurement demonstrates good governance of the IT assets. It also provides the CIO with solid evidence if she has to defend some elements of her department against the onslaught of third-party "low-cost" vendors.

This chapter continues to make the case for good IT value management.

Good value measurement

"If it cannot be measured it cannot be managed" is a widely accepted aphorism. Some work has been done in the area of IT value measurement, but I have yet to see a satisfactory approach to measurement that is both easy to capture and a genuinely useful measure of value. In respect of IT, value measurement often descends into cost measurement, as this is easier to measure, but of course it is not telling the full story. Here are some reasons why it is important to measure value accurately.

To justify having an IT department

It is in the IT department's interest to deliver the maximum return on your organisation's investment in IT. Demonstrating good value, as mentioned above, is critical if the CIO is to defend his empire against replacement by a third-party supplier. Third-party vendors – whether onshore, near shore or offshore – tend to be commercially astute. They recognise that the way to sell their services is to "dollarise" the value they will deliver should they be awarded the contract.

If the IT department is unable to demonstrate the value it delivers in a boardroom-friendly manner then, whether it actually delivers good value or not, it will be exposed to replacement by a third-party IT function that at the very least talks a good game. Similarly, by demonstrating good value, the IT department encourages the business to increase investment in new technologies.

At the shop floor level, the appraisal and development of the IT staff will be less arbitrary if one can measure individual performance in relation to the value each person delivers to the business.

To make the CFO feel in control

Information technology represents a significant percentage of an organisation's expenditure. The CFO is tasked with generating the maximum return on the corporate assets. Information technology assets tend to irritate the CFO because not only are they generally expensive to acquire, but they decrease in value quite rapidly. Worse still, the organisation typically underutilises these fast-depreciating assets.

It would be some consolation if the CFO felt that she had a handle on the value delivered by these assets. It would make authorising large payments destined for enterprise applications suppliers feel less like a religious act of faith. In a perfect scenario the CFO would receive metrics from the CIO that are expressed in monetary terms. But as we shall see, metrics expressed in dollars will not necessarily paint a useful picture. (However, if your CFO simply wants to know whether the IT department has provided the same service – whatever that might mean – as last year for less cost, then dollar metrics will do it.)

Chief financial officers who are focused on just driving down the cost of the IT function possibly need to become more aware of how IT can be used to increase shareholder value. It is worth noting that CIOs looking to advise the board in terms of the benefits of IT should keep in mind the sensitivity of the CFO in terms of IT value measurement. Thus the CIO is encouraged to position potential benefits in terms that enthral the CFO (though use of the word "prison" is also something of an attention-grabber).

To make the IT department staff feel valued

The lingering perception that IT doesn't deliver a good return on investment eventually impacts the self-esteem of those who work in the IT department. This dampens morale and ultimately leads to a substandard service, which in turn reinforces those perceptions. Those who work in the IT department need to feel they are in a noble profession that is at the heart of generating business value, rather than being part of an ancillary service that is in competition with other seemingly low functions to earn the title of "most reviled".

If the world is truly gravitating towards IT-centricity, and there is strong evidence to suggest this, then there will be a talent war to harness the world's best technologists. It is my view that in time the top technical architects will have their own agents, not unlike rock stars and sports heroes. If your organisation has a contemptuous attitude towards the IT department and IT staff, you will find that your best IT talent will gravitate to where they feel valued. Once the word gets around, you will find it difficult to replenish your IT gene pool. This will have a detrimental impact on your organisation.

So, good value management includes valuing your IT staff. Whilst it might seem tempting to leave this to the CIO, it is recommended that you actively manage and nurture your best technology talent, otherwise it will walk straight off your balance sheet.

To sweat the suppliers

Many suppliers enjoy the benefits of inefficient buyers. Good IT systems that enable the organisation to synchronise and lever its purchasing power will enable buyers to get best value from their suppliers. Centralised internal exchanges that enable staff to electronically purchase anything from staples to staff from a handful of competing vendors is all to the good. Electronic exchanges have still to deliver on the promises made during the dotcom era, but they do represent the future. Unsophisticated adopters of online exchanges will focus solely on price. Enlightened users will focus on value and will consider other criteria beyond price – such as quality of service, length of relationship and financial stability.

Information technology provides the tools to make one's supply chain more efficient. Increasingly this is an entry condition to competing in certain markets – in which case it is not so much delivering competitive advantage, though the absence of IT in managing the supply chain will certainly constitute a competitive disadvantage, not least in terms of cost and reliability. Be aware that the concept of demand chain management is causing even mature industries such as retail to revisit their supply chain technology. This raises the stakes in respect of both supplier management and supply chain management.

Because the customer wants to sweat you

Commoditisation is a characteristic of mature markets. So unless you deal in the "exotic", you will be feeling the firm downward pressure of your customers on your margins. Eking out a profit, despite the lower price/better service expectations of customers, is almost universally the new market model. The use of IT is critical to business sustainability under these harsh conditions. The value IT delivers can thus be categorised as business-critical. This of course links in to supply chain management as well as customer relationship management. The latter can be considered as the source of supply chain management activity.

To please the regulators

Regulators are not a new phenomenon. Recent high-profile corporate scandals have stimulated a new appetite for regulatory legislation, at least amongst governments and industry regulators. Today, regulators can be added to the list of stakeholders we have to please. They want to see governance controls and they want to see that these controls are reliable. These controls are usually implemented into business processes, which themselves are underpinned by IT. Hence, regulators see value in the use of IT because new technology provides a mechanism for delivering effective controls.

Overburdened regulators will look out for signs of poor governance and will focus their attention on those that exhibit the associated characteristics. Poor IT governance will attract their attention. Developing a reputation for extracting maximum value from one's IT investment is likely to cause your organisation to slip down the rankings of the regulator's watch list.

To ensure the users are supported in their roles

Users are an expensive element of business processes. Therefore there is a real need to sweat one's organic assets to ensure they deliver best value to the organisation. IT plays a key element in this. Ask any fighter pilot or investment bank trader – the better the technology supporting the user, the more effective they will be. So the more value one can extract from the IT investment, the more empowered the users will be. The more empowered the users are, the more likely they will deliver value over and above just being an organic cog in your organisation's business processes.

To ensure that the customers are delighted

Ultimately the value obtained from investing in IT needs to translate into business or customer value. There is a clear correlation between the value delivered by the IT investment and the value customers receive from patronising the organisation. Value perception may arise because of:

- Lower prices achieved through automated business processes.
- An improved online experience, where the web is used as a sales/delivery channel.
- Improved offerings brought about by the organisation's innovative use of IT.

Over time, customers will differentiate their suppliers in terms of the extent to which they lever IT to improve the customer condition; particularly where the only channel to the supplier is via the web. Under these circumstances, the online experience is everything.

To please the shareholders

Shareholders expect continuous value improvement from their investments. Most shareholders and potential investors recognise the power of IT to drive out costs and thereby improve margins. Smart investors recognise how IT can be used to:

- Enable the organisation to keep in tune with the changing marketplace.
  - A good indicator of sustainability.
- Sell deeper into the market through better customer intelligence.

Thus investors will expect their investments to lever IT for maximum bottom line impact. Organisations looking for investment will need to demonstrate that they have an IT-centric operation. Investors will increasingly see technophobic or techno-indifferent organisations as an investment risk. As existing investors become more tech-savvy, they will scrutinise the organisation's strategic IT-related initiatives – these being an indicator of future value growth.

If you want your organisation to be acquired then you will need to ensure that your IT assets are indeed assets rather than liabilities. If your IT management/governance is not delivering value then it is a business risk, which will erode your asking price.

To ensure the business doesn't become a basket case

At the opposite end of value enhancement through IT is business survivability. Very few organisations will be able to remain competitive in this increasingly real-time Darwinian era if they are not using IT. Given that new technologies are relatively expensive assets that depreciate rapidly, it is important that they deliver value that exceeds the cost of purchase and ongoing maintenance (aka TCO – Total Cost of Ownership). So, it is not enough to embrace new technologies. It is a basic requirement that substantial value is extracted from the investment. Otherwise, the IT investment becomes a corporate liability.

Poor use of IT will put your organisation at a competitive disadvantage. Failure to address this will drive your business to an early conclusion.

Rationale Summary

A cost-centric mindset is unlikely to yield the best return on one's IT investment. Those that focus on (as yet to be defined) value are more likely to reap real business benefits. Good IT value management requires positive action at all levels of the IT Value Stack. It also requires a measurement framework, along with continuous monitoring, to ensure that the associated value is translating into real business, and ultimately, customer value.

Stakeholders – including shareholders, employees and customers – will all benefit from improved IT value management, thus making it strategically important. The next section explores the issues obstructing the extraction of value from one's IT investment.

Value Management – Why it Doesn't Happen

Value is a perennial theme for twenty-first century organisations. Shareholders are focused on monetary return. Accordingly, organisations typically describe their value-add in such terms. Given the high percentage of organisational cost expended on IT, it is somewhat surprising that so little has been achieved in respect of IT value management. In this section we will explore why this is the case.

CFO focused on cost

One only has to look at the way company finances are presented to understand that cost is a major focus for CFOs. Non-financial concepts such as intellectual capital or IT value are nowhere to be seen. So if it isn't expressed as money, the CFO is unlikely to take an interest in it. Economic downturns reinforce this focus – the CFO moves centre stage in the business. Like a martial artist, swords in both hands, he slashes all around him. He devotes particular attention to costs that do not appear to be directly related to revenue. I have seen this taken to extremes where even the costs were cut on what were cost-cutting IT projects. Such indiscriminate cost cutting can work out quite expensive in the long run. But the flailing swords appear to give the CEO and other board members a warm feeling that the CFO will get them through this difficult period.

It is reasonable for cost cutting to be a theme of an economic downturn. But if we look to the sports industry, how many teams decide to reduce their investment as a response to poor performance? In any case, many CFOs have a money/cost outlook. The IT department's inability to present its value in these terms makes the CFO feel as if she is gambling whilst blindfolded when making IT-related financial decisions. So it is not surprising that the CFO takes a crude approach to handling IT spend.

The CFO needs to understand the value the IT department is delivering, even if it is expressed in non-monetary terms. Thus the IT department needs to present its value in a CFO-digestible form. Failure to do this will make it easier for the CFO to apply the scythe to IT spend. The IT department does not help itself when it embarks on projects without a sound business case. The apparent lack of synchronisation with the business objectives will make these projects an easy target for cost slashing.

In general, CIOs do not speak in CFO-friendly terms. This is a problem.

Alpha CFO

In many organisations the CFO is the designated boardroom representative of IT, even though he is unlikely to provide any operational or even strategic input into the IT department. Thus a CIO or IT manager is required to run the IT department on a day-to-day basis. This decoupling of power and responsibility is dysfunctional. In many organisations the CIO is thwarted because the CFO is ill-equipped to evaluate proposed initiatives.

The CFO can quite naturally feel insecure with this arrangement, which can lead to compensatory alpha (fe)male behaviour. This manifests itself in a number of ways, including:

- The CFO thwarting the CIO's business improvement initiatives.
- The CFO making technology decisions and driving them through the IT department regardless of technological or even organisational appropriateness.

Organisational seniority does not trump new technology expertise. And CFOs that think different are dangerous.

But to some extent the CFO should be alpha-like in their behaviour as should all the other board members. This creates vigorous debate at board meetings and usually leads to thought-through strategic business decisions. But there are two dangers here. The more general danger is when all the egos in the boardroom become aligned into one super ego that has its own interests at heart rather than those of the stakeholders. The second danger is more specific. The absence of IT expertise at board level will enable IT proposals to go unchallenged. So the CFO's recommendations may well get approval without proper scrutiny. At the very least the CIO should be on the board. Increasingly the other board members will need to develop sufficient knowledge of IT and its impact on business to counterbalance IT-related proposals.

Thus, the unchecked CFO is a risk to your business.

IT value is difficult to measure

The value delivered by purchasing a Rembrandt is difficult to measure, but we know that the buyer believes that in monetary terms it exceeds the purchase price. The value delivered in hiring a good waiter is again difficult to pin down. But as long as the restaurant delivers a healthy profit and no-one has complained about the new employee, the general feeling is that the waiter is good value. Perhaps if the waiter was able to demonstrate that he is a critical factor in diners visiting the restaurant then he might command a higher wage.

Similarly, how does one measure the value delivered by attending a newly released film? Some attend such films in order to gain greater social status. Having seen it first they are in a position to express their views to the less socially swift. Others might look at the film in terms of the volume of entertainment provided – i.e., the film's duration. So the more "film hours per dollar" received the better. Time-starved people will take the opposite view (up to a point).

So, value measurement is not always easy to measure. One has to choose performance indicators that are meaningful to senior executives. The decision to allocate your organisation's capital to a new business initiative is typically based on the return on that capital over and above what would be earned by leaving it sitting in the bank.

Information technology at the end of the day, is just another use of capital, so can we not apply the same principle? Yes, if we could isolate the value IT delivers. IT can be considered as a collection of asset classes as follows:

- Hardware.
- Software.
- IT department staff.

To what extent do we measure the value of each PC or the local area network? When do they start to deliver value, and when do they cease to deliver value? PCs, for example, also have the capacity to consume value by enabling users to self-generate problems that need to be handled by the IT department.

Both hardware and software are generally expensive assets to acquire. They also decrease rapidly in value. Worst of all, these assets are under-utilised.

I am certainly not stress-testing my laptop by using it to write this book. And whilst I sleep, the laptop will go through an extended period of zero utilisation. So even before we measure the value IT can deliver, we need to think about performance optimisation, before we make a value judgement.

Looking at the IT staff, how much value do they arrive with? Should we place more stock in their technical or business experience? Or even their business-friendliness? How do we reassess their value as they get "up to speed" in terms of their role? What if they become managers? All in all, IT value is difficult to measure.

But CFOs crave a numeric value. Cost is easier to measure than value, and in the absence of value information they quite naturally focus on cost. Thus, metrics such as IT spend reductions year on year or IT spend in relation to similar organisations prevail. Neither fit into an "IT as a tool for market advantage" framework.

Smart CFOs know that IT should be measured from a value perspective, but are thwarted by the challenges identified. Some of the major industry analysts have come up with value metrics such as total value of opportunity or total economic impact, but these do not really tell the full story. Should one consider IT value in terms of the MIPS per dollar (mega instructions per second – an indicator of processing power)? This only takes into account the value delivered by the hardware. How do we factor in software and technologists? Possibly the value IT delivers needs to be expressed in relation to the users or even the shareholders, though it would be unfair to hold the IT department responsible for shareholder happiness.

Information technology value measurement is in its infancy. A more reflective and easy-to-measure approach is required.

The IT industry doesn't understand business value

This is a generalisation of course, but from my experience it seems to be the norm. Not all IT suppliers understand the connection between their offerings and the needs of the buyers. There are several disconnects in the IT value chain that runs between buyer and supplier. The first is at the buyer–supplier interface. The vendor's sales representatives typically do not understand how to map their offerings onto the needs of their clients. So they are most comfortable selling at the operational level, where the focus is on the "what" (i.e., features, which can be read from a specification). Selling to managers requires an appreciation of the "how", as in "how will this offering help meet my quarterly targets?" This requires a more consultative approach. Fortunately for the sellers, today's buyers are not that sophisticated in respect of their IT procurement skills.

As mentioned, at a strategic level the buyer is interested in "why" they should allocate their capital away from other initiatives to what is being offered. This requires the business developer to have an intimate knowledge of his offering and the buyer. Such business developers are rare. Even where the business developer has the skills to ascertain the real needs of the buyer, the chances of this wisdom entering into the product development lifecycle are low. This is mainly because sales people are typically less interested in what might benefit the client next year. Sales commissions are based on now. The tension between the sales and marketing function in respect of tactical versus strategic market approaches means that this "captured" wisdom is lost. And even if it is captured, the product development people may not process the requirement in a timely manner due to an inflexible system development approach. Thus the supplier fails to capitalise on what the market wants.

These disconnects conspire to ensure that the IT industry fails to act on what the market is trying to tell it. Thus many IT offerings are suboptimal from a business value perspective.

Boardroom IT abdication

A recurring theme in this book is the need for the board members to take on their fiduciary role as IT leaders. That is to say, business leaders must actively engage in strategic matters relating to IT. There is too much trust and not enough verification. Many senior executives are not comfortable in dealing with IT-related business matters. Given that business matters are increasingly underpinned by IT, this is a worrying state of affairs.

The user–IT department relationship has never been an easy one. Much of the IT industry's evolution was driven by the power struggles between these two tribes. The users know they need IT but don't fully trust the IT department. The boardroom has handled this by effectively compartmentalising IT (and its associated issues) into a black box. That way they can spare themselves the detail, which if nothing else is a tidy approach to management. However, the absence of IT representation at boardroom level effectively renders the boardroom unable to make sensible IT-related business decisions.

One of the management team is usually assigned responsibility for IT. This typically falls to the CFO or some other multi-tasking senior executive. As mentioned, very few CFOs actually understand IT. Typically the CIO will manage the budget on behalf of the CFO and the understanding is that they will keep the lid down on the "black box". This model is like that of IT outsourcing, where it is the suppliers' job to deliver and how they go about delivery is their business. But outsourcing or any other purchasing of services only works when there is a knowledgeable buyer. Unfortunately, this is not generally the case, and this leads to an absence of strategic IT management.

Value proposition unclear

Human resources delivers business value through the staff. Marketing delivers greater customer reach. But what does the IT department deliver? Information technology value is not something that your stakeholders can readily appreciate. There is a vague sense that IT delivers value because it enables business automation and where it remains necessary to have staff, IT makes them more productive. But this could be said of electricity. So is IT really delivering any value over and above that of a utility?

We know for sure that there is no competitive advantage in using electricity, but there is certainly a disadvantage in not using it. Similarly for telephones, though the use of mobiles in one organisation may give competitive advantage over firms that do not issue them to their field operatives.

Word-processors, spreadsheets and browsers can be considered commodities, much like electricity. But a customer-friendly website with automated up-sell intelligence cannot be similarly categorised. Today, a trading system with in-built and up-to-date controls that support regulatory compliance is very value-adding, particularly if the boardroom makes the connection with possible incarceration. What is special today will be a commodity tomorrow in many cases. But the IT industry is young and so has many years to run before every aspect of IT is considered a commodity and so of limited value.

But there is a lingering feeling that much of what the IT industry offers and the IT department delivers cannot be linked to real value. The fact that IT value is so entwined with business value makes it difficult to isolate the value solely delivered by the IT department. Thus the quest for value is impaired. Organisations that resolve this today will have a greater chance of remaining in play tomorrow.

Problem Summary

As we have seen, there are a number of fundamental issues leading to the underperformance of IT in terms of value delivery. This applies to both the IT industry and the IT department. Notably, none of these issues has anything to do with technology per se. Of course, poorly architected systems are common, as are systems built on poor user requirements capture; both real value dampeners. But in my view these are symptoms rather than the cause of poor IT value.

Technophobic executives are part of the problem, as are the IT industry and its reseller channel (aka the IT department). Both are as yet unable to articulate the true value IT delivers to consumers of IT. Thus many IT-based business decisions are underpinned by vagueness and hope. The next section takes a look at how the IT industry and its customers can move away from this misty state of affairs.

Towards Value Management

This book is dedicated to improving the value business leaders distil from their IT investment. In the course of this book I have made a number of recommendations to that end. This section majors on the value measurement aspects of IT value management and touches on a number of board-level recommendations.

Become an IT leader

When we explored people management, we looked at upgrading the skills base and attitudes of the boardroom. As mentioned, a techno-indifferent/ technophobic boardroom culture will cascade down through the organisation. Disliking the IT department will, much like writing with a fountain pen or reading the *Financial Times*, be seen as a *de rigeur* characteristic of tomorrow's business leaders.

Attempting to tackle the development needs of senior executives may, on face value, yield results. A knowledge/attitude upgrade programme might appear to achieve its objectives. Business leaders may cease mocking the CIO by seeing how many pens they can fit in their breast pocket before he notices. It's a start. But the underlying resentment and fear may remain, so the boardroom may have simply evolved to techno-acceptant.

To truly increase the chances of the organisation getting best value from its IT investment the senior executives need to move beyond techno-acceptant to techno-inspirational. You should encourage your people to embrace IT and what it can do for your stakeholders, by setting an example. I have seen a marked change in some end-user organisations that were once traditionally slow followers in respect of new technology leverage. Having seen the light, their aspirant senior executives are pointedly involving themselves in IT initiatives in order to make their résumé cry out "tech-centred business leader in waiting". Rather than choosing to sidestep IT for fear of association, they are diving in, often making great mistakes, but most importantly gaining experience and confidence.

I encourage business leaders to round out their business profile by doing a stint in IT. Business leaders of tomorrow will not only have carefully steered their way through finance and/or sales, but through the IT department as well. Those who acquire IT scars in the course of their career will be very attractive to farsighted boardrooms. The CEO wants multi-talented individuals in the top team. For this reason the CIO is encouraged to spend some time in finance and sales.

Some national cultures will adapt quicker than others. Some cultures see technologists as a type of subclass. So any personal development that might make one a little more like a technologist will be avoided at all costs. Other, more forward-thinking cultures will soak up anything that makes them appear tech-savvy. Corporate cultures can similarly vary in this respect. The more "anti-tech" the culture, the stronger the IT leadership required.

The development of an IT leader requires the following:

- A fundamental understanding of IT terminology, issues and trends.
- An appreciation of how IT can be used to drive down costs.
- An appreciation of how IT can be used as a channel to the market.
- An appreciation of how IT can be used as a tool for business innovation.
- An understanding of the risks and the management of those risks associated with the adoption of IT.
- An understanding of how to win the respect of the technologists.
- An understanding of how to handle IT suppliers.
- An inspirational persona.

Not all of these can be addressed by the learning and development department. So the quest for excellent IT leadership needs to commence at the recruitment stage.

This talk of IT leadership is not an attempt to dissolve the position of the CIO. In an enlightened organisation the CIO will be the virtual chairman of the IT leadership team. In other words, when the board-room matters turn to IT, the CIO becomes the facilitator and final arbiter of IT-related decisions. It is the job of the IT leadership team to ensure that the IT department delivers business value. The key point here is that this responsibility arches both the IT department and the business. Again, IT is too important to be left to the CIO and the IT department.

Respect the CFO

Much of my earlier comments positioned the CFO as the bad guy. This is perhaps unfair because in some cases IT has been dumped on them, simply because it is a large cost to the organisation. In the absence of anyone understanding IT at board level, IT responsibility might as well be given to somebody that understands costs. The consequent "alpha" behaviour mentioned earlier is perhaps just a reaction to this unwanted responsibility.

Again CFOs, being cost-focused, are unlikely to get the best value from the IT investment. In my view this situation is made worse because all strategic IT matters are under the control of one person. This is further worsened by the fact that this person generally doesn't understand IT. But the CFO shares a trait with the CIO that is extremely valuable to the business. That is, they have an end-to-end view of the business. Their perspective is both strategic and detailed. On top of that they have the best handle on the financial health and sustainability of the business. For these reasons they make excellent CEOs.

It would be unwise for the CIO to look for revenge on the CFO as the tide turns back in their favour. The CIO has much to learn from the CFO in terms of leadership by numbers, and how to handle the labyrinthine world of stockmarkets, pension fund managers and mergers and acquisitions.

Proof of CFOs and CIOs working in partnership will one day be an indicator of business health. Hybrid CIFOs – i.e., those that have a deep understanding of both IT and finance – will be in a particularly strong position to contend for the position of CEO. Promoting a CIFO to the "top banana" position will indeed be a shareholder-pleasing event.

Take joint ownership

Just in case the point has not come across, I believe that the CIO must work with the rest of the executive team in respect of IT. Strategically impactful IT decisions need the approval of the management team. Similarly, the outcomes from these decisions are the joint responsibility of the management team. Operationally I have advocated treating the IT department as an internal service provider to the business. Financially I think this is a reasonable model. And from a service perspective it encourages good performance. Strategically the CIO, as trusted digital adviser to the boardroom, has to be the objective.

But in the real world the trusted adviser is generally a more sophisticated breed of sales person. So some CIOs might benefit from sales skills development. With this model there is a danger that the trusting buyer is happy to let the advisor make the important decisions. The trusting buyer thus needs to become the "trusting and verifying" buyer. The management team must be equipped to "push back" and probe the recommendations of the CIO. A good CIO will value this feedback and tune their suggestions accordingly. This healthy dynamic culminates in better decisions and thus more valuable outcomes. This requires technology confidence in the "non-IT" board members and technology humbleness in the CIO.

Perceived versus actual value

I mentioned the problem of value measurement. Most IT value measures are pseudo science designed to make the business leaders feel that IT is under control. Until IT becomes more science than art, a simpler approach is required. To understand IT value and the role business and IT plays in IT value delivery, I have coined the terms *perceived value* and *actual value*. Now to explain these terms.

I believe that if users (both internal and customers) are happy with what the IT department does for them, then the IT department is delivering value. "Happy users" will win the vote of many stakeholders. They will certainly see the IT department's service as valuable. But possibly their happiness comes at the expense of the shareholders. Beyond a certain point the increase in user productivity or customer spend is no longer proportional to the IT investment in user happiness. So it is possible that the IT department is using too much business capital – an element of the IT spend is underperforming from a capital return perspective. Ultimately this could drive the business into bankruptcy. With this in mind, I refer to the value delivered to users and customers as perceived value.

From an IT value perspective, having referred to perceived value, I now introduce actual value. Whilst perceived value relates to happy users and customers, actual value relates to happy shareholders. Generally speaking, the IT department can exercise considerable control over the IT experiences of users and customers and so it would not be unreasonable to entrust the IT department with delivering this perceived value. An upward trending share price is generally the key indicator of shareholder happiness. But shareholder happiness involves more than impressive IT delivery. All departments play a role in improving shareholder happiness.

Unfortunately the IT department cannot totally control how well the IT systems are used in support of the business goals. A great CRM system with a reluctant/incompetent user base in the sales department will yield a lower stakeholder value measurement than a great system and competent users. The same applies to all departments/business processes across the organisation. Thus it is unreasonable to hold the IT department solely responsible for the delivery of actual IT value. **This in turn leads to the crux conclusion of this book; the responsibility for delivering actual value from one's IT investment lies with everyone in the organisation.** That means users in general and business leaders in particular.

Once this message is understood, the race will be on to entwine the IT department into the business, rather than having it sit isolated in an ivory tower. Those that manage to fuse the "IT knowledge" gene into the business leadership will gain instant advantage. A better understanding of IT and its impact on business in the leadership community will very soon improve the organisation's investment in sales, marketing, manufacturing and so on. Excellence in IT is not the key objective. Excellence in sales, delivery and so on is. Thus the IT department needs to be aware both of its criticality to the organisation, and also of its relative importance in terms of strategic imperatives.

Make users happy

Making users happy is tough when distrust is the shared emotion of both technologists and users towards each other. Imagine a high-profile former mugger trying to brighten up your day by telling you jokes as you travel back home in an almost empty train carriage. Despite his seemingly good intentions, you are likely to keep your guard up for fear that he will revert to his old behaviour. Trust is way off the radar. Distrust to happiness is a long road. Much like rekindling a damaged relationship, the offended party needs to be respected. They need to determine the speed at which the relationship is repaired.

Information technology departments are encouraged to invest in public relations. Initiatives that reposition the IT department as user-centric, accessible, innovative and reliable will help. Most of all, actions that support these messages are needed. Fifty years ago information technologists were mad scientists so to speak. Highly technical individuals wrapped up in their own world. The simplification of technology today no longer requires this mindset or even intelligence. IT staff need to shake off the 'head in the clouds' uber-logician, and don the clothes of well-rounded business professionals.

Make customers happy

Customer experience is generally improving from an IT perspective. We have come a long way from the DOS prompt. Broadband and the World Wide Web have played their part, as has the influx of creative talent into the industry. Online services make customers feel empowered, which is a double result for the business as this removes/reduces the need to have customer service staff on the payroll.

There are still opportunities for improvement. Areas such as accessibility, security, navigation and data validation could be improved. We are moving to a browser-based world, and so the associated technologies used to build websites that are functionally more than just brochureware need to be chosen and implemented with care.

The IT department has an important role to play in supply-chain management. A more intelligent approach to logistics, procurement and manufacturing will drive down the cost of delivery. The customer will be happy if some of these cost savings are reflected in your pricing. They will be delighted if your supply chain provides them with more choice and greater customisation on top of lower pricing.

Make shareholders happy

Smart shareholders will be happy if they see that the IT department is fully entwined with the business. They will be happy when they see that every business function is using IT to be leaner and nimbler. A well-governed organisation with digital dashboards at every level of the organisation will give the shareholders comfort. As well as internal metrics, the capturing and monitoring of market metrics will give shareholders the sense that the organisation is adaptive. If your organisation is a "one trick pony" or focuses its mission statement around its products, you are unlikely to adapt to market changes. The demise of the dinosaurs is the oft-quoted analogy used to highlight the consequences of failing to adjust to the changing environment. Value-based shareholders do not want to invest in dinosaurs.

The IT department has a role to play in shareholder happiness, but only through working closely with the business functions.

Implement satisfaction measurement

Regularly surveying the stakeholders is critical to ensuring that the business is gleaning best value from its IT investment. I am no expert in surveys, but I would recommend that these are a mixture of quantitative (Score from 1 to 10) and qualitative ("How do you feel about . . . ?"). As well as directly requesting feedback, one should monitor indirect feedback. For example, number of helpdesk calls received, average resolution time, ratio of web visitors/buyers, number of newsletter subscribers and/or number of annual reports downloaded. As you would expect, 20 % of all possible metrics will yield 80 % of the information you need, so choose your metrics carefully.

Ensure the stakeholders know how you are doing. Feedback loops will help your organisation evolve. During the dotcom era many organisations created online forums to enable users to talk to each other. The aim in part was to get them to resolve each other's issues and thereby reduce the organisation's helpdesk spend. Some users saw the forum as a way to vent their spleen in respect of their poor customer experience. Panicking organisations shut down their forums; smart organisations kept them open and listened.

By taking the criticism "on the chin" and responding publicly in a humble and reasonable manner, these organisations demonstrated their respect for the customer community. This was also an effective way of handling vociferous extremists who were determined to "bad mouth" your organisation. Organisations that acknowledged and addressed their concerns politely, effectively made the complainant appear unreasonable, and so in the eyes of onlookers their complaint became somewhat diluted. In any case, regardless of the type of complaint or complainant, the open forum provides an opportunity for your organisation to demonstrate its values. And equally important it provides a mechanism for connecting to the real world, and learning how your organisation is perceived.

Organisms that learn from their environments are more likely to survive.

Action Summary

Strong IT leadership forms the bedrock on which to build a sustainable business in the twenty-first century. Understanding what IT value means and how to measure it is important. Gauging how happy the key stakeholders are is the easiest and most effective approach to establishing whether your IT investment is paying off. Happiness is indeed the path to IT enlightenment, though nirvana might be thought of as a state when there is a direct synergistic correlation between IT investment and share price.

Most important of all, the IT department cannot deliver IT value on its own. It is the responsibility of the business as a whole. This will be one of the most difficult cultural challenges many organisations will face. Those that do not address this challenge will find themselves in an uncompetitive state, though mercifully for only a relatively short period.

Value Management – External Perspectives

This section provides an alternative view to my own in respect of value management. The contributors were asked to answer one or more of the following questions:

- Why is value management important?
- Why is this not generally being addressed?
- What are the underlying problems?
- What are the consequences of failing to address this issue?
- What advice would you give in respect of value management?

Why is value management important?

> IT often is one of the most expensive functions. Understanding the costs and therefore the inherent value is a fair request by the business. Everyone wants to know what they are paying for.
>
> *Vivian Ash, Group Information Manager, BASF*

> No one likes to pay for something when they can't see the value it brings.
>
> *Karen Mellor, IT Capability Associate Director, Astra Zeneca*

> Without this the suspicion that IT are not optimising their budget will persist. Just because it is hard to measure does not mean that the organisation can avoid the associated dialogue.
>
> The business needs to understand what effort it takes to achieve change so that cost benefit cases are meaningful and intelligent choices can be made.
>
> *Philip Wright, Corporate Services Director,*
> *Standard Life Healthcare*

In a word, "credibility". IT needs to win the argument by demonstrating that it delivers and does so efficiently (however that is ultimately measured).

The maxim that you can only manage what you can measure is very applicable to IT value.

Richard Boreham, IT Strategy, Governance and
Performance Practice Leader, KPMG

Each department has to demonstrate its value. But to what extent do we gauge the value of the HR department, the facilities department, the legal department or any other department? Typically the value each one delivers is expressed in departmental-specific terms. So IT value management has to be expressed in IT terms, which is partly about keeping systems up and running and partly about contributing to and leading innovation.

Nick Leake, Director of Operations and Infrastructure, ITV

Why is this not generally being addressed?

Many managers regard IT as a necessary evil. They see corporate-wide IT initiatives as stifling innovation rather than helping it. The bigger the organisation the more IT has a subservient role. An IT portfolio that is light on strategic initiatives is unlikely to deliver high business value.

Karen Mellor, IT Capability Associate Director, Astra Zeneca

Measurement of operational KPIs is relatively straightforward. Measurement of value is tricky – contracts and SLAs go some way – payback periods/ROI is one way, but the business can be suspicious of such mechanisms.

Vivian Ash, Group Information Manager, BASF

Again it's quite difficult to do well and requires a long-term focus to develop meaningful information.

Richard Boreham, IT Strategy, Governance and Performance Practice Leader, KPMG

I think people are trying but there are obstacles to progress. In particular the absence of shared language, shared vision and shared strategy.

Philip Wright, Corporate Services Director, Standard Life Healthcare

You do not necessarily have to measure something to know its value!

Nick Leake, Director of Operations and Infrastructure, ITV

What are the underlying problems?

Poor relationships and misconceptions with what technology can do if used correctly. IT managers who focus on the technology rather than the business evolution are a source of value-related problems.

Karen Mellor, IT Capability Associate Director, Astra Zeneca

Simply the difficulty in "proving it" by numbers and statistics. If value is not obvious then measurement is just trying to prove something that in most cases the users will never buy in to.

Vivian Ash, Group Information Manager, BASF

- Industry comparative benchmarks are generally ineffective. This is because the statistics are often based on too small a sample and the collection processes are subject to skewing of data. Benchmarking does have a place but only for performance investigation. They can usefully identify areas for further investigation and management action.
- Benchmarking metrics are typically technology based. A cost per "mip" does not mean much to a business customer. They would prefer business measures (e.g., cost per current account serviced). Such benchmarks are not readily available. However, they can be created internally and used for ongoing internal benchmarking.
- Automation. When IT Management Information (MI) frameworks are put into place they are rarely done within the context

of the organisation's ability to collect and collate the information. This often leads to the creation of manual MI bureaucracies.

Richard Boreham, IT Strategy, Governance and Performance Practice Leader, KPMG

A lack of trust and understanding between users and technologists.

Philip Wright, Corporate Services Director, Standard Life Healthcare

Does it add value to measure the value of IT? If things are going wrong you know it from either a high cost base or poor levels of user satisfaction. You can sense/check these easily by seeking external advice/comparison/benchmarking.

Nick Leake, Director of Operations and Infrastructure, ITV

What are the consequences of failing to address this issue?

You are unlikely to be maximising the value you can receive from your IT investment.

Nick Leake, Director of Operations and Infrastructure, ITV

IT is not seen as a value-adding service, which reduces departmental motivations and recognition within the business. Bad news all round.

Vivian Ash, Group Information Manager, BASF

What advice would you give in respect of addressing this issue?

- Build partnerships.
- Provide core services.
- Ensure that key individuals are working alongside business leaders to bring in up to date technologies that support strategic direction rather than improving services that are already okay.

Impact analysis can help to identify services that are failing to deliver business value. Also establish what are the appropriate solutions. Sometimes a bicycle is required and sometimes a Ferrari. Ensure delivery is need rather than want-driven.

Karen Mellor, IT Capability Associate Director, Astra Zeneca

Employ a Service Delivery Manager – whose job description includes "proving" the value to the business of IT – but not with numbers (if at all possible).

Vivian Ash, Group Information Manager, BASF

A way for the IT executive to favorably impress senior management is through the use of marketing techniques to raise awareness of IT's value. This boils down to executive education.

A powerful use of executive education is in creating a "first love syndrome." Essentially, one can do this with any new strategic area that emerges rapidly, and as a result, triggers some anxiety on the part of senior managers. This anxiety usually stems from the need to be "in control" and to provide leadership to the organization, whilst at the same time not understanding what opportunity or threat the new initiative represents to the organization. The trick is for an IS organization to present the opportunity (e.g., Web, wireless) in a way that is relevant and meaningful to an executive audience.

Pete DeLisi, Founder and President, Organizational Synergies

- MI does need to be set up. We would always advocate a balanced scorecard approach here.
- Such frameworks are often best set up on the back of a performance improvement initiative, building metrics against the areas where you need to exercise control and make change.
- Internal benchmarking (year on year) is the best approach for trend monitoring. External benchmarking should be reserved for performance investigation within IT.
- A stepwise process is best (simple first and then getting more sophisticated) to prevent new bureaucracies and avoid added cost.

- For organisations that outsource, benchmarking remains a powerful tool for ensuring suppliers deliver service at a competitive value point.

Richard Boreham, IT Strategy, Governance and Performance Practice Leader, KPMG

Remember, finance has evolved its language since the 15th century heyday of Venice. It should not surprise us that IT is still little understood. We all have to work at this.

Philip Wright, Corporate Services Director, Standard Life Healthcare

IT Value and You – The Top 10

10

"There is nothing more difficult to take in hand, more perilous to conduct, or more uncertain in its success, than to take the lead in the introduction of a new order to things."

Niccolo Machiavelli, Political Philosopher

We have covered a lot of ground in this book. To turn the recommendations into demonstrable value requires action. My simple (but not easy) advice would be to take the recommended actions associated with each layer and implement as many as possible, starting at the strategy entwinement level and working up through the IT Value Stack. This approach is strongly recommended. But for those who simply cannot take such a systematic approach, I have distilled the contents of this book down into 10 "tactical" measures that will help you to get more value from your IT investment.

1. Consider IT Impact of Every Business Decision

There are very few business decisions that do not involve IT. Given IT's neurological relationship with the business, it seems unwise to ignore the impact of IT on business decision-making. Most organisations make a business decision and then inform the IT function that it needs to be supportive. Smart organisations will not make the decision until they have considered the impact of IT from a cost, risk and innovation perspective.

Business decisions have pulse-wave impact on the IT Value Stack, so consideration needs to be given to all seven layers, particularly if the decisions have strategic implications.

2. Consider Business Aspect of Every IT Decision

The converse is to consider the business reason for every IT decision. There should be a clear link between what happens in the IT department and its impact on the business. One might argue that the choice of the preferred in-house programming language has no impact on business, and so should be left to the IT department. Broadly speaking this is true. Infrastructural IT decisions are an IT department call. Application/services decisions ultimately are a business call. Creating/modifying an application without consideration of the impact on the service, processes and people in particular is likely to lead to a poor return on the associated IT investment. However, keep in mind that an IT decision to change the standard in-house programming language will have a business impact, if the IT department cannot find skilled staff to build business-critical applications at the clock speed needed by the business.

So in my view even infrastructural IT decisions need to take into account the possible impact on the business. The closer the decisions are to the services aspects of IT, the more important it is to consider the business implications. In addition if an IT decision has no business impact then why make it? There needs to be traceability between IT activities and business requirements.

3. Become IT-conversant

Most business–IT problems stem from poor communications. Business people and technologists are renowned for speaking different languages. So should the business people make the effort to understand the IT terminology or should the technologists talk IT in a business-friendly manner? In my view both are required. Business people need to understand not just the terms, but the associated risks and opportunities associated with the use of IT. An awareness of technological trends will enable business people to drive the IT agenda. Today it is often the reverse.

The IT department has generally been at war with the business for many decades and the changes in technology architectures over time tell the story of the power struggle between both tribes. But it is time to move on. Technologists must now engage with the business and work as a team. Everyone's survival depends on it. So technologists need to understand the business terminology and the business drivers, and be able to think in terms of profit, loss, risk, governance and prison.

The IT department is effectively a service provider, so IT people need to develop their bedside manner. This means talking respectfully to the users regardless of their IT competence. IT conversant thus means more than being able to talk IT, but being able to talk IT in a business-relevant manner.

4. Create an IT-centric Culture

An IT-centric culture is not one where everyone wears sandals and burns joss sticks. By IT-centric I mean that everyone in the business sees IT as core to their productivity, and the barriers – both physical and mental – that separate the business and IT communities are dismantled. This is a tall order. It requires the IT department to find the resources to embark on a charm offensive, backed up by a genuinely responsive and reliable service. The IT department needs the users to give it another chance to prove its value to the organisation. The end result is that business and IT people work in harmony to achieve the business objectives.

In this improved culture, the technologists determine business decisions as much as the users. The users thus need to be more tech-savvy and the technologists need to become trusted advisers. An IT-centric culture will mean that your organisation starts to "hunt as a pack" and "punch its true weight". In the medium term this will yield competitive advantage; in the long term it will be an entry condition to industry.

Smart organisations are recognising that IT is core business and so IT needs to be core to the culture. An organisation's attitude to IT will increasingly be a useful metric for potential investors.

5. Treat the IT Department like a Business

The IT department needs to stand on its own two feet and compete for its right to support the business. Hermetically sealing the IT department from the Darwinian world of business will "spoil" the IT department staff and ultimately damage your organisation.

The CIO should see this as an opportunity to prove that she can run a business. Becoming the next CEO will be less of a risk if the other business leaders know that she has both leadership and business management skills. The sooner in-house IT departments feel the bracing wind of competition, the sooner they will adapt to give the third-party outsourcing suppliers a run for their money.

Having discussions around service levels and value for money are more meaningful when the IT department has a commercial outlook.

6. Unclog the Arteries

Ensure that the critical data, information, knowledge and wisdom are accessible to those that need them, when and where they need them. The circulation of the corporate "lifeblood" is critical to being a market-sensitive on-demand organisation. Technology, both wired and wireless, provides the delivery mechanism, but is rarely the cause of clogged communications.

More often it is poor processes and empire-building humans who see other departments/lines of business as threats rather than colleagues.

A culture of cooperation is required. Those who contribute the most to, for example, knowledge sharing should be rewarded accordingly. Superstar sales staff that hoard information about their key contacts are a major threat to your business, as are "jobsworth" IT staff who enjoy the power rush of controlling access to company data. The converse is where the arteries are too free-flowing. Lax security profiles ensure that data are readily accessible to people who should have surrendered some of their access rights when they changed role.

Given the focus today on governance, whether via regulatory compliance or not, healthy arterial flow is critically important to ensuring that you and your colleagues retain the confidence of your critical stakeholders.

7. Define and Measure IT Value

Be sure that all IT stakeholders have a common definition of IT value. As I have suggested, it is tightly coupled with shareholder satisfaction and it would be appropriate to link IT value to profitability. A simple metric such as the gross profit divided by the IT spend (perhaps averaged over three years) will yield a crude figure that over time would be of value to the CFO and his colleagues. Again this highlights that the extraction of business value from one's IT investment is an enterprise-wide endeavour.

If value measurement is to be used purely as a tool to check that the IT department is performing, then polling the users and online customers and establishing their satisfaction levels in respect of IT will deliver the information that is required. Comparing IT spend for given periods can present a misleading impression, and also reinforces the emphasis on IT being a cost to manage rather than a tool for innovation. In any case, the price of technology is dropping and so one might expect to see a downward trend in cost for a given level of service. But keep in mind that labour costs are not following the same trend. There will be some short-term gains by using offshoring locations, but in keeping with globalisation and labour mobility the labour costs will even out across the planet, and will likely increase as the availability of high-quality labour skills fails to keep up with demand. Thus those CFOs looking for a drop in their IT costs over time are likely to be disappointed, and so this metric will be of little value, unless irritating the CIO is an objective.

8. Tame the Suppliers

Organisations are reliant on technology suppliers for the provision of IT. The IT department in this respect can be thought of as a supplier, or more accurately a value-added reseller. Thus suppliers are an important part of the IT eco-system. Their natural aim is to maximise their return. Slowly but surely the IT industry offerings are becoming commoditised. This is putting the buyer in the driving seat, but we are some way off complete commoditisation of the IT industry, particularly at the "big ticket" end. Exotic or single-source solutions empower the sellers. The buyer has no frame of reference in which to compare pricing. Other factors need to be considered. If the suppliers are not tamed then they will exploit the situation. This seems harsh on suppliers, but their behaviour is an instinctive response to weakness on your part.

The most effective way to tame the suppliers is for buyers to stop playing the victim role. That requires you to be sufficiently aware of IT and its impact on your business to defend yourself from the (sometimes) inflated claims of the supplier. To tame suppliers fully, insist that they understand both your business and their business before they try to engage with you. Failure on either point will lead to a waste of your time. Once the word gets around, suppliers will do their homework, and you will benefit.

Reward those clients who are prepared to invest in the relationship, particularly those that exhibit the characteristics of a trusted adviser. You need a consultative seller rather than a hustler.

9. Strengthen the Value Chain

To recap, the IT value chain runs from the supplier, through your procurement department, into the IT department. From there it either flows directly to the users via the web, or flows into the user community in the business. Hopefully the users are also using the IT systems to deliver business value to your customers. Each interface is a potential obstacle to the flow of value. So attention needs to be given to ensure that, for example, the IT department and the procurement department are on the same wavelength, or that users (e.g., the helpdesk) and customers speak the same language.

The flows may vary from one situation to another. For example, the acquisition of IT talent will include candidates in the supply chain, along with recruitment agencies and the HR department. Ensure your IT recruitment agency speaks the language of the candidates; otherwise, it will be a value-dampener rather than a value-amplifier in the value chain.

Invest in your own people to ensure they are IT value-amplifiers. Make it a requirement that suppliers can similarly communicate to their partners along the supply chain. Your value chain is only as strong as its weakest link.

10. Become an IT Leader

Leadership involves setting a vision and inspiring others to buy into the vision. Information technology leadership means creating a vision of an organisation that uses IT to be both lean and agile, and ultimately successful. Convincing techno-sceptics to buy into this vision will not be easy. In some cases it may be easier to jettison these people rather than trying to "reprogramme" them. At a practical level, IT leadership means creating an

IT-centric culture, where each person plays their part in sweating the IT assets, as proposed by this book. This means shaking up the status quo and redefining the responsibilities of your fellow business leaders.

Whether you focus on the positive, as in "embrace IT and take over the world" or "ignore IT and the organisation will collapse" you will only be a successful leader if your people are tuned for IT followership. Inspiring talks will wash over reluctant listeners. The people in your organisation need to be developed to a level whereby they can understand your message. Good IT leaders will invest in making their people good IT followers.

Summary

Many of the top 10 actions advocated here will have a shock-wave impact on the culture of your organisation. Anticipate the backlash and approach these actions accordingly. They will absorb a significant amount of senior executive time. There will be a great temptation to abdicate this to the IT department or to even to ignore it.

If you envisage IT as being akin to one's nervous system, then failing to address the issues highlighted by this book will in effect increase the chances of your organisation suffering corporate Alzheimer's. Your inability to respond to market changes in a synchronised manner will become increasingly frustrating and will ultimately result in corporate demise. Addressing the neurological aspects of your business today will give it a fighting chance of thriving in the future.

Businesses generally take a short-term outlook. Business leaders who take up the challenge must understand that they will not necessarily enjoy the full benefits of their toils during their tenure. But what a legacy to leave behind. Those that have the vision to anticipate the future and act on it today are indeed truly great leaders.

Over to you.

ABOUT THE CONTRIBUTORS

To give this book balance, I have incorporated the perspectives and insights of respected individuals in the world of IT. I am grateful for their efforts and their wisdom. Details of the contributors and their employers follow. Please note that the views expressed by the contributors in this book are not necessarily those of their employers.

Vivian Ash   Vivian Ash is Group Information Manager at BASF plc. BASF plc is the UK and Ireland operational division of the Global Chemical and Pharmaceutical company BASF AG. His responsibility is to coordinate the IT demand management with vendors and providers, as well as to formulate the strategy and delivery of IT initiatives within the business. Many companies view IT as an overhead to be handled with caution. Vivian's objective is to endeavour to make IT a competitive asset, embraced by management and users alike. **BASF** is the world's leading chemical company. its portfolio ranges from chemicals, plastics, performance products, agricultural products and fine chemicals to crude oil and natural gas. BASF has approximately 94,000 employees, customers in over 170 countries and about 150 production sites.

Richard Boreham   Richard Boreham – BSc(Hons), MBA, Chartered Engineer, member of the British Computer Society – leads KPMG's IT strategy, governance and performance business. Richard has 20 years' experience in IT delivery and management, spanning financial, commercial and public sectors, including: retail banking, insurance, fund management, utilities, central government ministries and large spending agencies. Richard is a keen yacht racer. **KPMG** is the global network of professional services firms that provides audit, tax and advisory services. KPMG LLP operates from 22 offices across the UK with 9000 partners and staff. KPMG LLP, a UK limited liability partnership, is the UK member firm of KPMG International, a Swiss cooperative.

Robina Chatham Dr Robina Chatham qualified as both a mechanical engineer and a neuroscientist. Robina subsequently followed a career in IT, which culminated in the position of European IT Director for a leading merchant bank. In 1996 Robina joined Cranfield School of Management as a lecturer in management information systems where she created the acclaimed programme – Organisational Politics and IT Management. In 2000 Robina authored her book "Corporate Politics for IT Managers: How to Get Streetwise". Robina now runs her own training company, Robina Chatham Ltd, and is also a Visiting Fellow at Cranfield School of Management. **Cranfield School of Management** is one of Europe's leading university business schools. Established in 1967, it is renowned for its high-quality teaching and research and strong links with industry and business. The Information Systems Group at Cranfield is the largest of its kind in the UK.

Rumi Contractor   Rumi Contractor joined HSBC in 1987 and has worked with various entities in Buffalo, New York, Hong Kong, London, India and Brazil. He became Chief Information Officer for HSBC Technology Services UK and Europe in October 2005. Rumi is married to Carla and has two teenage daughters. His interests include reading, motorcycling and learning languages. **HSBC** Holdings plc serves over 125 million customers worldwide through some 9500 offices in 76 countries and territories in Europe, the Asia-Pacific region, the Americas, the Middle East and Africa. HSBC is one of the world's largest banking and financial services organisations. HSBC is marketed worldwide as "the world's local bank".

Pete DeLisi   Pete DeLisi is founder and president of Organizational Synergies, a strategy consulting firm. He is also the Academic Dean of the Information Technology Leadership Program at Santa Clara University in Silicon Valley, California. **Organizational Synergies** is a "new age" consulting firm that focuses on the unique dynamics that underlie contemporary organisational problems. It lies not in the singular specialty that historical consulting firms have brought to the table, but rather, in the unique intersection of multiple disciplines, such as, strategy, culture and IT.

Shaun Fothergill   Shaun has worked within the IT industry for the last 24 years. His career spans all aspects of IT from software to hardware. Over recent years, he has focused upon the key issue of IT and business alignment. His research has shown that to a large degree the real issue

IT and businesses has is a lack of a real "language" of understanding. He has worked with businesses internationally. He has provided alignment advice within all aspects of IT and business, particularly in the areas of security and compliance. He is a regular contributor to the press and has run interactive workshops at conferences worldwide. **CA** offers customers the greatest breadth and depth of IT management solutions and services, based on best practices and proven processes. CA is the global leader in enterprise IT management.

Rob Fraser

Rob Fraser is a member of the Boots Executive team and IT Director for Alliance Boots Health and Beauty division, Europe's largest health and beauty retail chain with over 1700 stores. Rob led the team that delivered the three-year, £350M transformation of Boots' IT systems. An Engineering graduate from Balliol College, Oxford, prior to Alliance Boots he worked for Marks & Spencer and Arthur Andersen Business Consulting. Rob is married with twin daughters. The merger between Boots Group and Alliance UniChem created an international pharmacy-led health and beauty group operating in more than 15 countries (including associates) across the world. **Alliance Boots** offers a strong combination of pharmacy, pharmaceutical wholesaling, wholesale, retail, acquisition and brand management experience. It is Europe's leading health and beauty retailer.

Andrew Holmes

Andrew Holmes is a director with PricewaterhouseCoopers. He has a background in IT, programme management and finance effectiveness. Andrew has consulted with national and international clients across a range of industries. He has written 12 books on a wide spectrum of business topics, including why IT projects fail and technology management. The member firms of the **PricewaterhouseCoopers** network provide industry-focused assurance, tax and advisory services to build public trust and enhance value for its clients and their stakeholders. More than 130,000 people in 148 countries across their network work collaboratively using Connected Thinking to develop fresh perspectives and practical advice.

Nick Leake　Nick Leake is Director of Operations and Infrastructure at ITV. Nick joined Carlton TV in 1997 from a career in management consultancy in the media and broadcast sector and a period in Bell Canada's UK Cable TV operation. Within Carlton he had responsibility for IT across all TV operations and was responsible for turning around a failing group into an externally recognised leading UK IT function. Nick has an honours degree in computational science from the University of St Andrews in Scotland. **ITV** is Europe's largest commercial broadcaster and the UK's most popular family of TV channels, making many popular and well-known programmes. Based in London, the organisation was formed in 2004 from the merger of Carlton Communications plc and Granada Media plc.

Sam Lowe　Sam Lowe is a Sector Chief Technology Officer at Capgemini UK, and a board member of the Enterprise

Architecture practice. He specialises in advising clients on IT strategies, architectures and key technology use. He also advises on business relationship improvement and collaboration, IT governance and operating models. This has involved working with a large number of blue chip companies, covering many industries including Retail, Consumer Products, High Tech, Life Sciences, Media and Financial Services, and speaking at many public and client events. **Capgemini** is one of the world's foremost providers of consulting, technology and outsourcing services. It employs approximately 61,000 people worldwide. It has a unique way of working with its clients, called the Collaborative Business Experience, based on its network of world-leading technology partners, collaboration-focused methods and through its commitment to mutual success with its clients.

Goretti McCormack-George

Goretti McCormack-George is a senior manager with Deloitte, and has been with the firm since 1991. She played a key role in the formation of the IT department and the early development of Deloitte's IT infrastructure. Apart from supporting Deloitte IT Operations in Dublin, Cork and Limerick, she also works closely with the IT Team on project implementation. **Deloitte** Ireland is a world-class firm of expert business advisers, serving senior business leaders who are seeking to protect and create value in a complex, dynamic environment. Their objective is to help their clients succeed by anticipating tomorrow's agenda with focused, insightful and fresh thinking born out of their multidisciplinary strengths. They draw upon their specialist skills in audit, tax, consulting and financial advisory both within Ireland and across the Deloitte worldwide network.

Karen Mellor

Karen Mellor is IT Capability Associate Director for Astra Zeneca. She currently works on developing individual and organisation capabilities in line with business drivers and strategy. She is primarily concerned with the development of an agile IT workforce that is able to shift focus in line with changing business trends. **Astra Zeneca** discover new medicines that are designed to improve the health and quality of life of patients around the world; medicines that are innovative, effective and which offer added benefits such as reduced side effects or better ways of taking the treatment. They also focus on getting the best from every medicine they make by exploring all the ways it can be used or improved.

Karen Price

Karen Price, OBE, is the CEO of e-skills UK. Karen's early career was in education prior to a wide-ranging career in business, including directorships in the construction and publishing industries, leading company start-ups, and also holding a number of roles in IBM UK's Corporate Affairs and Global Services divisions. Karen led the mergers that created e-skills UK in 2000, and the licensing of the company as a Sector Skills Council in 2003. Karen was awarded an OBE in 2006 for services to the IT industry. **e-skills UK** is the employer-led Sector Skills Council for IT and Telecoms, and part of the Skills for Business Network. Its mission is to unite employers, educators and government to ensure the UK has the technology-related skills it needs to succeed in the global economy. e-skills UK provides advice, services and programmes that have a measurable impact on IT-related skills development in the UK.

Heidi Sinclair   Heidi Sinclair is Burson-Marsteller's CEO for Europe. Heidi joined Burson-Marsteller as a Senior Vice President. In 1996, Heidi served as Managing Director for International Creative Management. In 1998, Heidi co-founded and served as CEO of BrandX Media, Inc. and in 2001, Heidi returned to Burson-Marsteller to lead the technology practice. **Burson-Marsteller**, established in 1953, is a leading global public relations and public affairs firm. It provides clients with strategic thinking and programme execution across a full range of public relations, public affairs, advertising and web-related services. The firm's seamless worldwide network consists of 55 wholly-owned offices and 46 affiliate offices, together operating in 59 countries across six continents. Burson-Marsteller is a part of Young & Rubicam Brands, a subsidiary of WPP Group plc, one of the world's leading communications services networks.

Laurence Trigwell   Laurence Trigwell is senior director of financial services solutions at Cognos. Mr Trigwell brings more than 20 years' experience in the financial markets, ten years of which were spent at Dresdner delivering business solutions across the investment bank. Prior to joining Cognos in 2003, Mr Trigwell was with Thomson Financial as Product Marketing and Strategy

Director, responsible for developing and executing product strategy for their suite of financial information and trading products in EMEA and the Asia-Pacific region. **Cognos** is the world leader in business intelligence and performance management solutions. It provides world-class enterprise planning and business intelligence software and services to help companies plan, understand and manage financial and operational performance.

Steve Tyler

Steve Tyler is UK Programme Director for LogicaCMG. He is a member of LogicaCMG's UK management board. Prior to this he was LogicaCMG's UK Technical Director. His background is in project and programme management. He has managed some of the company's largest and most difficult fixed-price contracts across most of the sectors embraced by the business. **LogicaCMG** is a major international force in IT services. It employs around 40,000 people across 41 countries. LogicaCMG's focus is on enabling its customers to build and maintain leadership positions using LogicaCMG's deep industry knowledge and its track record for successful delivery. The company provides business consulting, systems integration and IT and business process outsourcing across diverse markets including telecoms, financial services, energy and utilities, industry, distribution and transport and the public sector.

Ketan Varia

Ketan Varia, founder of kinetik solutions, has over 17 years of management and consulting experience, focused in leading and sustaining process improvement within an industrial/operational context. He has led change assignments for a variety of FT Global 500 companies including Abbey, BAE, EMI Music, Land Rover, Motorola and Xerox. Ketan previously worked for Ernst & Young and Capgemini. **kinetik solutions** delivers process-driven organisational change.

Philip Wright   Philip Wright is the Corporate Services Director at Standard Life Healthcare, one of the UK's leading private medical insurers. In this role his responsibilities include all IT systems as well as human resources and facilities. He is also leading a major business integration project. Philip's previous roles at Standard Life Healthcare include Sales Director, and he also has extensive experience in marketing. **Standard Life Healthcare** is an award-winning private medical insurer, and one of the largest providers in the UK. It supplies a range of healthcare plans to corporate and individual customers. As well as helping people to access the treatment they need at a time convenient to them, its products also support the health and wellbeing of its customers – it focuses on wellness, not just illness.

GLOSSARY

Actual value   The value shareholders receive from your organisation's
                    use of IT.

Application   This key element of information technology can be
                    considered as a user productivity tool. Organisations
                    get value from their IT systems through the use of
                    applications.

Asset   Something of value to the organisation that, if managed
                    carefully, may even increase in value. Such assets include
                    people, technology, capital and intellectual property.

Business   A term that refers to the tools and activities
intelligence   associated with generating useful information from the
(BI)   data stores in one's business.

Business process   The act of changing the existing business processes to
re-engineering   improve the way in which the organisation conducts its
                    business.

CEO   Chief executive officer. The person charged with manag-
                    ing the executive team and delivering shareholder/stake-
                    holder value.

CFO   Chief finance officer. The person charged with manag-
                    ing the assets of an organisation and ensuring good

accounting practices are in place. Often charged with managing the IT function.

CIFO — Chief information and finance officer. A notional role whereby the CFO is actually qualified to lead the IT function.

CIO — Chief information officer. The person charged with managing the IT budget.

Circulation — This is a term that relates to the movement of lifeblood (i.e., data, information and knowledge) around the organisation. Critical for management, governance and detecting market trends.

Corporate governance — The act of ensuring that a corporation's assets are managed carefully for the benefit of all stakeholders.

Customer relationship management (CRM) — A philosophy that is underpinned by the belief that it is easier to squeeze money from existing clients than to waste resources chasing new ones. This philosophy has driven the creation of many databased applications that support the management of customer data.

Demilitarised zone — A term used to describe the notional "no man's land" that sits between the IT department and the users. This land is usually occupied by analysts acting as emissaries to the parties on either side.

Digital coach — This concept encapsulates the need for technical people to guide business people in respect of their understanding of IT terms, trends and the impact of IT on business.

Globalisation	A term used to describe the fact that we all live in one global market and are thus subjected to global competition. Offshoring is a consequence of globalisation.
Governance	The act of ensuring that organisational assets are managed carefully for the benefit of all stakeholders.
Infrastructure	This is a collective term for those technologies that support the delivery of applications to the user.
IT governance	The act of managing one's IT assets such that their value is maximised for the benefit of all stakeholders.
IT value chain	This concept relates to any supply chain that involves IT. It is used in the context of people rather than technologies. Ultimately, such chains should deliver real business value.
IT Value Stack	The model created to help organisations get best value from their IT investment. It underpins this book.
New technology	An alternative term for information technology. New technology is also synonymous with digital technology.
Offshoring	Offshoring is a form of outsourcing where the associated activity is carried out in another country; usually another continent. Sometimes offshoring does not involve third parties. On these occasions the organisation concerned establishes a presence in another country in order to reduce its (labour) cost base.

Outsourcing

An approach to managing risk and cost by using a third party to manage elements of your business activities.

Perceived value

The value users and customers receive from your organisation's use of IT.

Prison

A secure environment, which is increasingly used to provide business leaders with time for reflection should they veer too far away from good governance.

Process

A unit of repeated activity in an organisation. Breaking business activities down into processes makes it easier to focus on critical activities and refine them, or at least reduce their associated cost.

Regulatory compliance

A term used to describe the act of ensuring that one's organisation is adhering to the rules applied from an external body, such as a government or industry body. As well as demonstrating compliance, one is usually expected to demonstrate that a framework is in place to ensure that compliance will be ongoing.

Risk

Something that may negatively impact your plan. Risks can originate from a variety of sources, including people, finance, time, technology and governance.

Service

The delievery of tangibe/intangible offerings that in some way improve the condition of the recipient. These are usually encased in some form of support aggrement. In respect of IT, service relates to the delivery of applications that enable users to do their job more efficiently when and where required. It also includes the associated support required to keep these applications available, secure and up to date.

Service level butler

A concept that takes service level agreements from the organisational to the personal.

Strategy

A plan of action based on one or more goals. Usually over a period of at least one year.

Techie

A term used to describe a person who works in the IT department and has a genuine understanding of how technology works. Unlike other terms used for technologists, techie is almost a term of affection.

Techno-acceptance

A condition whereby individuals understand what IT can do for their organisation but for whatever reason do not buy into the fact that IT is becoming more important to the organisation.

Techno-indifference

A condition whereby afflicted parties do not see the value that IT can deliver to their organisation. This is a dangerous condition because it can cause patients to behave as if they understand IT and its impact on their business. Often it is just a masking behaviour for the increasingly less acceptable condition known as technophobia.

Techno-inspirational

An enlightened state whereby individuals recognise that the future sustainability and success of their organisation is underpinned by the innovative use of IT. Such people are evangelical about this and so feel the urge to sell this vision to others. Ironically, technophobics are the most inspirational once they have made the transition.

Technology	Technology in general relates to something that came into existence through engineering endeavour, such as the car or the sowing machine. Typically today and certainly in the context of this book, when one talks of technology the understanding is that one is actually talking about new technologies, i.e., information technologies.
Technophobia	A condition whereby any contact with new technologies lead to uncharacteristic nervous behaviour. In severe cases merely discussing IT issues can trigger this condition. A "glazing over of eyes" is another common symptom.
Trusted adviser	This concept relates to a harmonious state whereby the advisee genuinely trusts an advisor, and so the former is more likely to respect and adopt the recommendations put forward by the latter.
User	A term used to describe a consumer of new technologies.
Value	A concept that relates to the return one receives from an investment over and above the costs associated with that investment.

INDEX